DAILY READINGS FROM THE BIBLE

**NEW**

# Dayl

CW00363032

*Edited by Shelagh Brown*

**The Bible Reading Fellowship**
OPENING THE BIBLE

# Writers in this issue

**Adrian Plass** is an internationally popular writer and speaker. In 1994 BRF published *The Unlocking: God's escape plan for frightened people*, which has been translated into German, Dutch and Swedish. It is now available in an updated edition and on audio-cassette.

**The Reverend Canon David Winter** was formerly Head of Religious Broadcasting at the BBC. Now a priest in the Diocese of Oxford and a regular contributor to Thought for the Day and Prayer for the Day, he is the author of BRF's best-selling Lent book *What's in a Word?* His most recent BRF title is *Forty Days with the Messiah*.

**Rosemary Green** works with Springboard, the Archbishops' Initiative in Evangelism and is the author of *God's Catalyst*.

**The Reverend Graham Dodds** is now the Lay Training Adviser and Director of Studies for Readers in the Diocese of Bath and Wells.

**The Reverend Marcus Maxwell** is Rector of St John's, Heaton Mersey in Lancashire.

**The Reverend Shelagh Brown** is Editor of *New Daylight*, a commissioning editor for BRF, an NSM in Weston-on-the Green, Oxfordshire, and a writer. Her most recent books for BRF are *Confirmed for Life* (with Bishop Gavin Reid), *Value Me* (with Phil Lawson Johnston) and *Feeding on God: discovering God through the whole of life*.

**Dom Henry Wansbrough, OSB** is Principal of St Benet's Hall Oxford, a writer, broadcaster, and General Editor of The New Jerusalem Bible. He was recently nominated by Pope John Paul as a member of the Pontifical Biblical Commission, which has just twenty members from around the world.

An obituary of **Prebendary Douglas Cleverley Ford** is on page 14 of *The BRF Magazine*.

All the writers in this issue are contributors to the *Day by Day* series. For details see the order form on page 159.

# THE BRF
# *Magazine*

# The BRF Prayer

*O God our Father,*
*in the holy scriptures*
*you have given us your word*
*to be our teacher and guide:*
*help us and all the members of our Fellowship*
*to seek in our reading*
*the guidance of the Holy Spirit*
*that we may learn more of you*
*and of your will for us,*
*and so grow in likeness to your Son,*
*Jesus Christ our Lord.*

# A Message from Her Majesty Queen Elizabeth The Queen Mother

CLARENCE HOUSE
S.W.1

As Patron I am so pleased that the seventy-fifth anniversary of the Bible Reading Fellowship is to be celebrated in Westminster Abbey on 30th January 1997. This underlines the fact that for the greater part of a century a society has existed to encourage people to read the Bible.

Familiarity with the knowledge imparted by the Bible is the receipt for leading a life of rectitude in accordance with the word of God. It is worth noting that many of the evils which beset us today would be avoided by strict adherence to the precepts of the ten commandments. In the New Testament can be found the words of Christ which contain the essential teaching for leading a spiritual life.

In happier days when everyone went to Church and children attended Sunday School these precepts became part of everyday life. Now, it is largely through the work of the Bible Reading Fellowship that people are led to follow the path which will lead them to fuller life in this world and the hope of eternal felicity.

ELIZABETH R
Queen Mother

January 1997

# The Editor writes...

We have suffered a real bereavement in the death of Douglas Cleverley Ford. He will be greatly missed by the readers of New Daylight and by all of us in the BRF office. You will find an obituary on page 14 of the *Magazine*—and the last notes in this issue are the last ones he ever wrote.

They are amazingly apt, because (except for the first two and the last one) Douglas wrote them just a few days before he died and went to glory. The final note is a reprint of the one he wrote three weeks after his wife, Olga, died. It was for 24 October 1994, and when it was published he received over a hundred letters from New Daylight readers, expressing their sympathy and saying how much his words had touched them. Douglas and Olga are together now, in the nearer presence of God, whom they both loved.

Easter comes in this issue of New Daylight, with its glorious reminder that because he loves us so much God-in-Christ died for our sins on Good Friday and was raised to life again on Easter Sunday. For the believer death isn't the end. It is the door to life in all its fullness. That life starts on this side of the grave. Jesus defines it in John 17:3, as he prays to the Father in the week before he dies. 'And this is eternal life, that they may know you, the only true God, and Jesus Christ whom you have sent.' Yet although we know him now, and love him now, our life is like a piece of music in a minor key, with a counterpoint of sorrow always playing even at the height of our joy.

But it won't always be like that. In the Revelation to John he is given a vision of heaven, and he hears a loud voice from the throne saying:

'See, the home of God is among mortals. He will dwell with them as their God; they will be his peoples, and God himself will be with them; he will wipe every tear from their eyes. Death will be no more; mourning and crying and pain will be no more, for the first things have passed away. And the one who was seated on the throne said, "See, I am making all things new."'

With my love and my prayers,
*Shelagh Brown*

# Richard Fisher writes

**H**appy New Year! On behalf of all of us at BRF may I offer you our warmest greetings and best wishes for this new year. 1997 is a very special year for BRF as we celebrate our 75th Anniversary, and we are particularly delighted to be able to include in this issue of the *Magazine* a special Message from Her Majesty Queen Elizabeth The Queen Mother, who has been Patron of the Fellowship since 1952.

BRF has come a long way since the first leaflet of Bible readings was produced by The Revd. Leslie Mannering for his congregation in January 1922. We hope that you will share with us in celebrating and giving thanks to God for all he has done over the years in and through BRF, its trustees, staff, authors and of course the hundreds of thousands of men, women and children throughout the world who have been helped by its Bible reading notes and books.

## You can play your part!

Many readers have approached us to ask what they can do to help promote BRF and its ministry during this anniversary year. The answer is very simple! If you think that the Bible is important, that it is relevant to Christians in 1997, that through it God still speaks to us today, and if you yourself are a regular Bible reader (and the very fact that you're reading this publication suggests that the answer to all these questions is 'Yes!'), then please join us in encouraging others to read it for themselves. Without doubt the most effective means of encouraging others is through personal recommendation.

Why not tell a friend, colleague, neighbour, family member why you read the Bible, how you read it, the resources that you use. You never know, you might get them started on a habit of a lifetime!

## Disciple

By the time you read this you may already have heard about *Disciple—Becoming Disciples through Bible Study*, an exciting new initiative which is now available in the UK through a partnership between The Foundery Press and BRF. You will find more details about *Disciple* on page 12.

## Large Print New Daylight

It was with regret that we had to increase the price of the large print version of *New Daylight* in September last year. As it became evident that we could no longer sustain the level of subsidy required,

7

the choice that faced us was either to increase the cover price and so reduce the amount of subsidy needed, or discontinue the publication and thus deprive nearly 2,000 subscribers of their daily notes. The decision seemed obvious to us, and in fact the price increase (of £1 per copy, effective September 1996) was the first since the large print version first became available in September 1992.

## Special Projects News

Last year we sent some books to ministers in Papua New Guinea and were overwhelmed and humbled by the letters of thanks and appreciation which we received from them. It made us realize afresh just how much we take the availability of books and resources for granted.

We hope to be able to do more to equip those in ministry in situations where either books are unavailable or in short supply, or where funds for obtaining them are limited. The response from those subscribers with whom we shared this idea last year was very encouraging. The funds donated for this purpose have enabled us to send more books to the ministers in Papua New Guinea, and to give further quantities of BRF books and notes for use in ministry among prisons in the UK. It is our hope that during this anniversary year we will be able to expand this work even further, so that ministers and pastors may be better equipped for their biblical teaching and preaching ministry.

## Lent

For many years now BRF has published a new book(s) each Lent. All of these follow the pattern of a Bible passage (printed in full), comment and prayer for every day from Ash Wednesday to Easter Sunday. Most contain questions for group discussion as well. Extracts from both new books for Lent 1997 are included in this magazine. Do ask at your local Christian bookshop, or contact us direct for details of other BRF Lent titles.

## And finally

Thank you once again for all your support for BRF. We look forward to seeing many of you at the Service of Thanksgiving in Westminster Abbey on 30 January, and at the other events during the course of the year.

PS You will find the Gift Subscription and Order Forms at the back of the notes.

---

### CORRECTION

In this column in the September–December 1996 issue of *New Daylight*, there were two instances where reference was made to 'readers of *Guidelines*', when instead it should have been 'readers of *New Daylight*'. This was due to a copy-editing error and we wish to apologise for any confusion and offence which this may have caused.

# 75th Anniversary Update

To remind you of what is happening and give you new information regarding events and initiatives for the year...

## Service of Thanksgiving and Rededication

Thursday 30 January 1997 in Westminster Abbey, London at 12 noon. A few tickets may still be available—contact Westminster Abbey direct for these.

## Group Secretary Days

If you are a Group Secretary you should have received details of these with this issue of the notes. If for some reason you haven't received them, please contact the BRF office for details.

## Pilgrimage to the Holy Land

There may still be places available. For further details contact the BRF office direct.

## Christian Resources Exhibitions

Come and meet BRF authors and staff, find out more about the work of the Fellowship and see the latest new publications.
20-23 May 1997 Sandown Park, Esher, Surrey
23-25 October 1997 G-MEX, Manchester

## Bible Sunday

An outline service, drawing from the Service of Thanksgiving in January will be available later in the year. Full details will be included in the September-December 1997 issue of the *Magazine*.

## Author Tour

A major author tour is planned for October. Look out for more details in the next issue of the *Magazine*.

## Information Pack

This is now available, containing ideas and suggestions for what you might do in your own church or area to celebrate BRF's anniversary and to promote and encourage Bible reading. Contact the BRF office to request your copy.

## Video

Regretfully we have had to postpone the planned video about BRF, but hope very much to be able to produce it at a later date.

## Souvenir Brochure

A souvenir brochure for the 75th Anniversary is in preparation. Further details to follow.

# New Hymns
## for BRF's 75th Anniversary

Bishop Timothy Dudley-Smith has written two new hymns to mark the occasion of BRF's 75th Anniversary. These new hymns will both receive their world premier at the Service of Thanksgiving and Rededication in Westminster Abbey on 30 January 1997.

We are delighted to be able to reproduce both hymns in this issue of *The BRF Magazine*. We hope that you will include them in any services of celebration and thanksgiving for BRF's ministry which you may be planning to hold in your own churches during 1997.

### God in his wisdom, for our learning

98 98 98
*Suggested tune: Fragrance*

God in his wisdom, for our learning,
  gave his inspired and holy word:
promise of Christ, for our discerning,
  by which our souls are moved and stirred,
finding our hearts within us burning
  when, as of old, his voice is heard.

Symbol and story, song and saying,
  life-bearing truths for heart and mind,
God in his sovereign grace displaying
  tenderest care for humankind,
Jesus our Lord this love portraying,
  open our eyes to seek and find.

Come then with prayer and contemplation,
  see how in Scripture Christ is known;
wonder anew at such salvation
  here in these sacred pages shown;
lift every heart in adoration,
  children of God by grace alone!

© *Timothy Dudley-Smith*

# Teach us to love the Scriptures, Lord

86 86 (CM)
*Suggested tunes: Contemplation, Westminster, Abridge,*
*St Hugh, St Timothy*

Teach us to love the Scriptures, Lord,
   to read and mark and learn;
and daily in your written word
   the living Word discern.

Your purposes in us fulfil
   as we your promise claim,
who seek to know and do your will
   and learn to love your Name.

When in some dark and cloudy day
   beset by fears we stand,
your word be light upon our way,
   a sword within our hand.

As on your word our spirits feed
   through all its pages shine;
make known yourself to us who read,
   the Bread of life divine.

So shall the treasures of your word
   become as sacred ground;
teach us to love the Scriptures, Lord,
   where Christ is surely found.

© Timothy Dudley-Smith

# DISCIPLE

## Becoming Disciples through Bible Study

'**I**f you make my word your home you will indeed be my disciples' (John 8:31, New Jerusalem Bible).

Disciple is an exciting new initiative now available in the UK through the partnership of The Foundery Press and BRF. Throughout the USA, South America, Australia, Germany, and Korea Disciple has been instrumental in transforming both individuals and entire congregations as they have worked through the course.

While so many churches seem to be more concerned with making *members*, Jesus was concerned with making *disciples*. Disciple provides a framework for people to relate the teaching of the Bible to their discipleship today, equipping them to serve Christ more effectively in whatever circumstances they find themselves both within and outside their congregations.

What is Disciple? Disciple is a 34 session course comprising daily reading assignments for the individual participant (approx 30 minutes reading per day) plus a 2½-hour weekly group session. The model for the group is twelve members

*One minister described Disciple as 'the course I have been looking all my ministry to find.'*

plus a leader, who is there as a leader/participant, rather than a leader/teacher.

Disciple requires a high level of commitment from both leader and participants. It is not to be entered into lightly, but has been found to be immensely rewarding by those who have taken part. In the UK a number of pilot schemes have been completed during the last two years, and all involved have spoken of how much they have gained from the course. One minister described Disciple as 'the course I have been looking all my ministry to find.'

Disciple takes the Bible as the text for study. During the course of the 34 weeks participants will read almost 70 per cent of the Old and New Testaments, large sections of which may be for the first time. There are 16 sessions on the Old Testament, one on the intertestamental period and 15 sessions on the New Testament. The final two sessions are for identification of ministry and leadership roles and for celebration of Holy Communion.

For many Christians, their knowledge of and exposure to the Bible is limited to small sections—fragments—the few verses a day in their daily notes, or the reading in church on Sunday. Disciple provides a framework for the reader to understand the broad sweep of the Bible—the 'big picture'. It takes us through the biblical story from Creation to the New Jerusalem, the unfolding story of God's relationship with his people. Each week a different 'Mark of Discipleship' is considered as we relate the themes and implications of what we are reading to our discipleship today.

Each member of the group has a study manual which includes all the daily reading assignments, along with commentary and questions for reflection and response. At the weekly study session the group will watch a video segment which comprises a presentation relevant to the week's study from an acknowledged expert in the field. This is followed by an exploration of the Bible passages which have been read during the preceding week. This will draw on the notes, insights and reflections which participants have recorded during their own reading. A short refreshment break follows after which there is an in-depth study of one passage drawn from the week's readings. Participants are introduced to a number of different Bible study approaches over the 34 sessions and discover techniques which they will be able to apply elsewhere in their own Bible study. Finally the group meeting ends with a consideration of the week's 'Mark of Discipleship' (see above).

*Each one of us in the group found ourselves gaining new insights into familiar stories and passages*

Many have asked how Disciple fits in with or relates to the popular Alpha course, which so many churches are now using to great effect throughout the UK and in more and more countries overseas. In our view Disciple and Alpha sit ideally side by side. Alpha is an excellent resource for evangelism and outreach which explains what the Christian faith is all about. Disciple enables people who are already Christians to go deeper into the Bible and to explore issues of biblical discipleship. Ideally churches would offer both courses!

On a personal note, I would not be prepared to promote Disciple had I not actually participated in a Disciple group myself. Between *continued on page 18*

# Prebendary Douglas Cleverley Ford

**D**ouglas Cleverley Ford died on 4 May 1996. He was a much loved contributor to *New Daylight* from 1989 until his death—and his last notes appear in this issue. When he wrote about the death of his wife, Olga, he had over a hundred letters from people expressing their sympathy and saying how how much that particular note had helped them. You will find it on the last day of this issue of *New Daylight*.

Obituaries appeared in *The Times*, *The Telegraph* and *The Independent*. The following is an extract from the latter, by The Right Reverend The Lord Coggan.

'During a ministry of nearly 60 years he served his generation well—mainly in four spheres.

'The first was as a parish priest... he built up the congregations by the excellence of his preaching... by his insistence on good music, and by his pastoral skill. People knew that if they went to him, especially if they were in trouble or perplexity, they would find a listening ear and an understanding mind. They knew

> *He did more than any other man of his generation in raising the standard of preaching in the Church of England.*

that they mattered—to him and to God.

'Secondly, he worked as a theological college lecturer and as the first Honorary Director of the College of Preachers... Many hundreds of clergy as well as Readers have him to thank for his care, for the lucidity of his lectures, and for the renewal of their preaching work. He did more than any other man of his generation in raising the standard of preaching in the Church of England.

'The third sphere in which he excelled was as senior chaplain to the Archbishop of Canterbury (1975–80). During my years in that office I benefited greatly from his work... He had a shrewd assessment of character. He was loved by the the staff at Lambeth, and his secretaries would do anything for him.

'His fourth skill was as a writer. Over many years, he wrote prolifically, bearing in mind those to whom he had lectured. He desired to enable preachers to do their work with honesty and enthusiasm and to enlist all the help at their disposal in making preaching what it is intended to be—intelligent, interesting, down to earth. The influence of his writings, however, went far beyond the men and women in the pulpit. Through his books...

through articles, through the notes he constantly wrote for the Bible Reading Fellowship, he reached many thousands of readers.

'As a man, he was quiet. Like the Servant in Isaiah, he did "not cry, nor lift up, nor cause his voice to be heard in the street". He did not need to. Some would say he was reserved; but those who knew him best enjoyed his deliciously keen sense of humour which lightened many a difficult situation.'

Douglas will be very much missed by BRF readers.

*Shelagh Brown*

---

Douglas Cleverley Ford often wrote notes on the Psalms for *New Daylight*, and shortly before he died BRF published his *Day by Day with the Psalms*.

'The Psalms grew out of life,' he wrote in his introduction, 'and life as we know it is never smooth for long. So the experience of God which they share with us is fragmentary, earthy and human. But as a result we can come alongside the Psalms. We can feel them, sing them and sigh over them... The Psalms are distillatons of life—its joy, its wonder, its laughter, its pain, its loneliness and its fear. They are about living and about dying. It is no wonder they have lasted so long. They have never worn out and they never will.

'The aim of this book is to help the Psalms to address our own individual and contemporary condition, and above all to sharpen and deepen our awareness of the real presence of God in the bitter-sweet knocking about which we know as life.'

# The Vision of God (part 3)

*Joy Tetley*

The biblical presentation of God is kaleidoscopic rather than definitive. The more we look, the more the patterns change. That leaves us in our proper place: wondering; grappling with poetry, mystery and paradox rather than presuming to try and control the great enigma who is God. To try to control God is to try to make ourselves greater than God. That is the primal human sin. And it seriously distorts our vision of who God is.

In safeguarding God's uniqueness, mystery and freedom, the biblical record, when speaking of God, is full of checks and balances. Not least among these is the rich variety of imagery used by the biblical writers. Their metaphors for God are strikingly diverse, often tumbling over one another in a way that throws up many perspectives, many questions. The God of the Scriptures will not be pinned down—except, briefly, on a Cross.

But that dark moment is, in reality, God's brightest beam of light. The God who is beyond our comprehension goes to extremes to make himself known. In a disfigured victim, battling to the end against pain, evil and death, is the focal self-revelation of God—a God whose love for us means more than life itself.

But there is more. As St John puts it, 'in the place where he was crucified there was a garden' (John 19:41). Gardens seem to be significant in the biblical record of God's dealing with us. According to Genesis, human life began in a garden. So did human deceitfulness. There are hints in Revelation of a garden in the city of fulfilment—suggested in the fruitfulness of trees bordering on the river of life (Revelation 22:1–2). And between beginning and ending, we find, for example, cultivated gardens where desire has been aroused (Song of Songs 4:15–16), and cultivated areas where God is portrayed as the gardener (John 15:1).

Now, in what seems the most unlikely place to produce any vision of God, opposite extremes are somehow brought together. Somehow the place of stark horror becomes the place of new life and fruitfulness. Out of darkness and suffering is born a new beginning. This Easter garden, grown out of evil and anguish, is far more fertile than primal Eden. Here love triumphs over hate, forgiveness breaks through the negative spiral of vengeance, joy emerges through pain, life conquers death—not in wishful thinking, but in God's reality. In that reality we can all share; for God does not keep his life to himself. He invites us into it.

It is Christ crucified who takes our pain seriously. It is Christ crucified who, with tortured hands, opens the gate of glory. It is Christ crucified, risen and ascended who ensures that our precious and brittle humanity is for ever at the heart of God.

To this God let us open our eyes anew. Let us 'look to Jesus.' Let us 'see' Jesus. Let us share Jesus. For, as the preacher of Hebrews so powerfully asserts, 'seeing Jesus' means looking into God's life. 'Seeing Jesus' means not only recognizing the presence of God, but being drawn into a face-to-face and heart-to-heart relationship with God. And that also means judgement, in its most radical, and ultimately positive, sense.

Seeing Jesus brings the truth to light—the truth of God and the truth about ourselves. In such mutual openness, we discover the reality of our salvation. We discover that we are loved and forgiven; more—that we are invited to be lovers of God. We discover that our wounds, meeting with God's wounds, can not only find understanding and relief, but even become a source of blessing—for others as well as for ourselves.

We discover that in God's eyes, we have enormous potential for creativity and joy; that, as partners of God, it is our duty, our delight and our travail to bring the best out of all that is; that in the enormity of existence, we matter. As Paul puts it, writing to the Church in Corinth, 'It is the God who said, "Let light shine out of darkness", who has shone in our hearts to give the light of the knowledge of the glory of God in the face of Jesus Christ' (2 Corinthians 4:6).

And what strange glory: hidden, vulnerable, yet carrying the unlimited power of absolute love. Tellingly and typically, the most

*Somehow the place of stark horror becomes the place of new life and fruitfulness.*

profound insight into this glory comes from the most unexpected quarter. As Mark so shockingly reminds us, it is a pagan outsider, one who is not a member of the chosen people, one who has none of the advantage of discipleship, one who is, quite literally, instrumental in crucifying Jesus, who, in facing this tortured figure dying in less than silent agony, perceives the presence of God.

God grant that we, to whom much has been given, may have the nerve and the strength to affirm that insight. And to go on to share the biblical vision of God with others, in the conviction that this God is powerfully and fundamentally on our side. Being open to such a God is the prelude to transforming grace.

*Joy Tetley*

*Joy Tetley has written* Hosea–Micah *in the People's Bible Commentary.*

---

*continued from page 13*
October 1995 and June 1996 I led a pilot Disciple group with twelve members of my own Anglican church in Oxfordshire. It was a fascinating and exciting journey. Each one of us in the group found ourselves gaining new insights into familiar stories and passages, and discovering parts of the Bible that we had never read before. The sense of anticipation as we came to read Matthew's Gospel in the light of sixteen weeks spent focusing on the Old Testament was almost tangible. And one of the most important things that members of the group without exception felt Disciple had given them was the overview, the framework, with which to understand, approach and explore the Bible. Quite simply, the time spent with Disciple is an investment for life, and wherever you are in your Christian faith, Disciple will equip you for a journey with the Bible that will last the rest of your life.

Disciple is not available through retail outlets. Churches must enrol in the programme and the enrolment fee includes two days' residential training for the group leader, along with all the materials necessary for the first group of twelve to study Disciple. For further details of the course and the training seminars planned for 1997, please send an A5 sae clearly marked 'Disciple' in the top left hand corner to BRF in Oxford.

*Richard Fisher*

Look out for BRF's brand new resource for holiday clubs:

# THE ULTIMATE HOLIDAY CLUB GUIDE

The school holidays provide an ideal opportunity to open your church to children of all ages at a time when they are most likely to be at a loose end and looking for entertainment for themselves and their friends.

Holiday clubs are a popular way to use the opportunity to the best advantage. They can be run on a scale to suit your church and the help you have available. But how to start? It's easy to be frightened off by the thought of keeping youngsters occupied, interested and coming back for more.

Here's an ideas-packed guide with all you need to get your holiday club going with a bang. It contains all the information you need to prepare, plan and put together a full programme of events based on a variety of biblical themes—the ideas spring from a wide number of field-tested ventures—plus three complete ready-to-run themes. So whether you are a large inner-city church or a small rural chapel, looking for fresh ideas or on your own wondering where to start, there is something here for you.

The authors have both had extensive experience in working with children at Christian camps and clubs. **Alan Charter** is a full-time youth and children's worker in a busy parish. He met **John Hardwick** whilst working on the Saltmine Children's Team. John has a unique combination of gifts and skills—unicycling, juggling, clowning, music and story-telling—which he uses to present the good news of Jesus Christ imaginatively in ways which appeal to children of all ages.

*The Ultimate Holiday Club Guide* puts everything you need to know at your fingertips, ready to leap off the page and into your church. Just add a pinch of planning, a dash of enthusiasm, then fill with kids and bring to the boil!

## WHY? WHERE? WHAT? WHEN?

A comprehensive section on running a holiday club including:
• initial planning
• roles and responsibilities check list
• using the Bible
• using visual techniques
• using music
• using your imagination
• following up.

## HOW to do it!

Three complete holiday club themes, each containing five full days of material including:

- setting the programme
- crafts
- games
- puppetry
- clowning
- theme illustrations
- serial dramas
- creative narrations of Bible passages
- theme songs
- memory verses
- funsheets with photocopy permission
- sheet music.

### The Big Top

Five power-packed days exploring the characteristics of God; looking at God's strength, God's love, God's power, God's faithfulness & God's leadership.

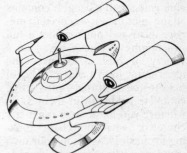

### The Adventure Cruise

Five fun-filled days on the high 'C's; exploring Choice, Call, Change, Commitment & Cost.

### Starship Discovery

Five life-changing days with Peter; exploring Turning, Trusting, Tripping, Transforming & Training.

## THE ULTIMATE HOLIDAY CLUB CASSETTE

Contains all the songs and memory verses for the three themes. Ideal for use during your club or as a learning resource, and for your children to take away with them as a memento of their holiday club experience. Side One contains all the songs, Side Two the backing tracks, to help you create that 'singalong-live' atmosphere if you don't have your own musicians.

At BRF our aim is to help *you* help your children to grow with the Bible. We hope you'll find the *Ultimate Holiday Club Guide* and cassette a resource to use and to come back to.

---

*Barnabas, an imprint of the
Bible Reading Fellowship*

The Barnabas imprint from BRF provides resources to help children under 11 years of age explore, enjoy and begin to learn from the Bible.

---

To obtain a copy of *The Ultimate Holiday Club Guide*, or copies of the cassette, contact your local Christian bookshop or use the order form on page 159.

# The Christian Life
## Beginning at the End: the Way of Prayer which Jesus taught us

### Simon Barrington-Ward

## 1. Our Father

Whenever Jesus meets with people, whether in the Gospel stories or now, amongst our contemporaries, he opens up a new possibility. There is such a strong positive sense of being loved and forgiven that you can be overwhelmed by an urge to throw in your lot with his kingdom community and to follow him. Every clause of the prayer which he taught us starts out from this sense of being grasped by God's overwhelming love and thus made ready, like St Paul, to reach out to grasp that for which Christ Jesus has already grasped me (Philippians 3:12).

At the outset, Jesus in Luke's version sets the single word 'Father'. This seems so like him. He immediately invites us to join him in that intimate, trusting relationship with God which he expressed in the word 'Abba', used by children in speaking to their father. This was his most intimate cry to God overheard in the Garden of Gethsemane in the midst of his agony (Matthew 12:24). He must have dwelt within this word himself. In this naked dwelling, he endured utter godforsakenness on the cross to break through death to a release of the Spirit into the hearts of all who turn to him, so that we too can confidently cry with him 'Abba'.

Matthew embellishes it with the traditional 'Our' and 'in heaven' to remind us that it is the prayer of the new covenant community, now held in unity with God.

All our prayers should start with remembering God's great love for us to which we are brought home through Jesus by the Spirit. We start by dwelling on this thought. It is then that we can long and struggle to become what we truly are.

## 2. Hallowed be your name...

As we really dwell in that sense of being loved and accepted just as we are and brought home to God, thankfulness and praise can well up from us. We want to be caught up into heaven in praising him and to see the world charged with his glory. We have arrived at the end. Heaven and earth are one and all creation shouts its praise.

But then again our joy is turned into longing. May your name be made holy. The prophets longed for this and felt that God's name was profaned through the failure of his people to live their praise out. (Isaiah 29:23, Ezekiel 36:23). Jesus prayed 'Glorify your name!' (John 12:28). But he knew that that prayer could only be fulfilled in the face of the failure of God's people in a sinful world if he were to lay down his life so as to raise up a new people. We too can only pray this if we are willing to take up his cross in our lives.

## 3. Your Kingdom come, (Your will be done, on earth as in heaven).

Again when Jesus prays this prayer the kingdom of heaven, the sovereign rule of God over everything, seems to be at hand. We begin to picture it. The torn creation made whole. A new kind of human society. A community, and even our own hearts united with God. Matthew amplifies the prayer again by adding 'Your will be done in earth as in heaven' and we remember once again that Jesus prayed this prayer in Gethsemane, 'Nevertheless not my will but yours' (Matthew 26:39). Only through our surrender and repentance can this prayer, fulfilled already in Jesus, begin to be fulfilled in us. Once again we move from the joy of the picture of the kingdom close at hand in Jesus to the yearning that God's will might be done not only in him but in us. We can pray then another very early version of this clause, 'May your Holy Spirit come upon us and cleanse us...' As our repentance for our own failure and

our intercessions for the world fuse into one great longing, so we seek to open ourselves to the presence of the Holy Spirit who alone can begin to fulfil this prayer.

## 4. Give us today tomorrow's bread...

Here Matthew's version has that original ring. The mysterious word translated in our modern versions 'daily', *epiousion* really means 'for the morrow'. It could be a prayer to rest secure tonight knowing that tomorrow's bread was there. But there is an echo of the manna that fell in the desert, when God gave enough for two days to cover the Sabbath. The Sabbath itself being a sign of the end time and the last day. There is a glimpse too of the feeding of the five thousand which was both a memory of the manna and an anticipation of the final feast of which Jesus often spoke. The bread of the morrow must be shared bread, bread broken in a longing for Jesus' coming. Each meal becomes, as for Quakers, a sacrament. We enter into the final feast already, but also we must struggle to share amongst each other bread and all material things if w are to know the joy of our true fulfilment to come.

## 5. Forgive (remit) us our debts, as we have forgiven our debtors...

Here too we are, thanks to the passion and death of Jesus, freed from sin and brought into that final state in which all is being forgiven and

23

forgiving. We have passed beyond the judgment, from death to life and into universal love. 'We have forgiven' our debtors already. There is a kind of general amnesty, a jubilee in which all sin has been cleansed away. And yet again we are not there yet. We need still to be grasped by forgiveness and also to be reaching out to forgive. Forgiveness is all we have. It is the central theme of the kingdom community. It is the way to the kingdom. That is why Matthew attaches such importance to this clause. Only through continuous forgiveness, love for our enemies, the love that drives out fear, can humankind reach its final fulfilment in God.

## 6. Lead us not into temptation (but deliver us from the evil one)

In this prayer, held in God's presence and love and in the final joy, we are secured and taken beyond the greatest temptation of all, to lose hold of God. We are taken beyond the trial of tragedy and suffering and death which can detach us from faith at the crucial moment. 'Suffer us not for any pangs of death to fall from you!' In Matthew's extra clause we pray to be delivered from the evil one, which is surely the more authentic and earliest reading. Our vulnerable little community of love prays to be protected from the mystery of iniquity and the great

*Forgiveness is all we have.*

destruction constantly let loose in this world. We are held in a love which 'bears all things, believes all things, hopes all things, endures all things'. And yet, paradoxically we must keep reaching out in faith to God in Christ or we shall lose that delicate poise of grace.

## 7. Doxology

It is surely true to the prayer that some ancient manuscripts in Matthew's version, as in the later document called the 'Didache' or 'Teaching', add 'for yours is the kingdom, and the power and the glory, for ever. Amen', with it strong echo of Judaic tradition, especially 1 Chronicles 29:11. This, though not part of the original, surely returns us to the end, which we know already as we dwell in God's love and rest in faith and hope. 'The last thing is a joy, a joy that rejoices out of an ever new joy in eternity.'

In all our prayer and life in Christ we learn to dwell in the end which he has won on his cross, the end which is now and not yet, and so to reach out for it daily. We cry 'Glorify your name, bring your kingdom, let your will be done in us.' And as we seek these things, we are led through shared bread, forgiven and forgiving and a constant deliverance, towards the still unseen fulfilment of our prayer.

# Searching for Truth

## From the introduction to John Polkinghorne's book

### A Scientist's Approach

Whatever it is that we do in life, the experiences we have will colour our thoughts and mould our ways of thinking. I have spent thirty years of my life working as a theoretical physicist, trying to use mathematics to understand some of the beautiful patterns and order of the physical world. For good or ill (and no doubt it is a mixture of both) this affects how I think about all sorts of things. The way I like to characterise my habits of thought is to say that I am a 'bottom-up' thinker.

What I mean by that is that I like to start with the phenomena, with things that have happened, and then try to build up an explanation and an understanding from there. 'Start with particular cases and only then try to go on to understand what's happening in general' is my motto. If you're a 'top-down' thinker, you like to go the other way: start with some grand general ideas and use them to explain particular events.

Bottom-up thinking is natural for a scientist for two reasons. One is that we are looking for ideas which have reasons backing them up, and these reasons will lie in the evidence we consider, the events that motivate our belief. The second point is that we have learnt that the world is full of surprises. That means it is very hard to guess beforehand what the right general ideas will turn out to be. Only experience can tell us that. In fact, this element of surprise is one of the things that makes scientific research worthwhile and exciting. You never know what you'll find round the next corner.

Let me give you just one example of these scientific surprises. Every day of my working life as a theoretical physicist I use the ideas of quantum mechanics. This theory describes how things behave on a very small scale, the size of atoms or even smaller. It turns out that the behaviour of the very small is totally different from the way we experience the world on the feet-and-inches scale of everyday life. We seem to live in a world which is reliable and picturable. We know where things are and what they are doing. All that changes when you get down to the level of atoms. Take an electron, one of the constituents of an atom. If you know where it is, you cannot know what it is doing; if you know what it is doing, you cannot know where it is! (This is called Heisenberg's uncertainty principle.) The quantum world is fuzzy and unpicturable. We cannot imagine in everyday terms what it is like. Nevertheless we can understand it, using mathematics and the special set of quantum ideas which we have learnt about from a bottom-up approach to atomic phenomena.

No one could have guessed beforehand that matter would behave in this very odd way when looked at subatomically. In fact it took many extremely clever people twenty-five years to figure out what was happening. If you want to understand nature, you have to let the physical world tell you what it's like. You have to start at the bottom, with actual behaviour, and work your way up to an adequate theory.

Now, if the physical world is so full of surprises, it would be strange if God didn't also exceed our expectations in quite unexpected ways. Commonsense thinking by itself won't be adequate to tell us what he's like. We'll have to try to find out from how he has actually made himself known. That's why I was keen in the preceding section to think of the Bible as a source of evidence about how God has acted in history and, above all, in Jesus Christ. It's a natural strategy for a bottom-up thinker to pursue.

You'll see, in fact, that I find there's a lot in common between the way I search for truth in science and the way I search for truth in religion. People are sometimes surprised that I'm both a physicist and a priest. They think there's something odd, or maybe even dishonest, in the combination. Their surprise arises because they don't realize that truth matters quite as much in religion as it does in science. There is an odd

view around that faith is a matter of shutting one's eyes, gritting one's teeth and believing impossible things because some unquestionable authority tells you that you have to. Not at all! The leap of faith is a leap into the light and not into the dark. It involves commitment to what we understand in order that we may learn and understand more. You have to do that in science. You have to trust that the physical world makes sense and that your present theory gives you some sort of idea of what it's like, if you are to make progress and gain more understanding and a better theory. You'll never see anything if you don't stick your neck out a bit! You have to do the same in the religious quest for truth. We shall never have God neatly packaged up. He will always exceed our expectations and prove himself to be a God of surprises. There is always more to learn.

There is one important difference, however, between scientific belief and religious belief. The latter is much more demanding and more dangerous. I believe passionately in quantum theory, but the belief doesn't threaten to change my life in any significant way. I cannot believe in God, however, without knowing that I must be obedient to his will for me as it becomes known to me. God is not there just to satisfy my intellectual curiosity; he is there to be honoured and respected as my Creator and Saviour. Beware! Let me utter a theological health warning or, rather, promise: 'Reading the Bible can change your life'.

26

# The Apple of His Eye

## An extract from the BRF book by Bridget Plass

### John 11:28–29, 32–35

*After she had said this she went back and called her sister aside. 'The teacher is here' she said 'and is asking for you.' When Mary heard this she got up quickly and went to him... When Mary reached the place where Jesus was and saw him she fell at his feet and said, 'Lord if you had been here my brother would not have died.'*

*When Jesus saw her weeping and the Jews who had come along with her also, he was deeply moved in spirit and troubled. 'Where have you laid him?' he asked. 'Come and see Lord,' they replied.*

*Jesus wept.*

Why? Why did he weep? Surely he knew that everything was going to be all right for his favourite family?

Was it because he felt guilty that he could have prevented their pain by coming earlier but because he needed Lazarus' healing to be a major miracle they had had to suffer? Or because he knew that what he was about to do was the beginning of his own long journey towards death? Or because he knew, as God's Son, that whatever he said they could not understand. Or quite simply because he was truly man while he was with us and couldn't bear to see his dear friends in such agony. Whatever the reason I'm so very glad he did.

Sometimes, especially since being a parent, I've found myself in a situation where I've known that someone's grief will only be temporary. I've plastered grazed knees and tried unsuccessfully to mend favourite toys; I've cuddled to sleep a toddler devastated by the loss of a one eared rabbit, I've attended funerals of budgies and hamsters; I've watched helplessly the agony caused by the betrayal of a best friend who chooses to sit next to someone else on the coach; I've touched fingers in sympathy at an unsuccessful audition; I've listened to the thudding grief of a small mud plastered footballer who has just scored an own goal. And I've been there myself.

I've learnt slowly that passing on knowledge that their grief will be temporary in the form of 'Never mind. You'll get over it' is useless and can be damaging. Yes the pain will lessen in time, may even go completely. But right now they are hurting and they can't understand and nothing will ever be the same again.

If you are in that situation now, needing arms round you and needing to know that someone who loves you is sitting in the dark with you, remember that Jesus wept. He knew he was going to heal Lazarus, but still he wept. He will never minimise your pain. Just as he was asking for Mary who had shut herself away from everyone in her grief, so he is asking for you. Let him weep with you.

## PRAYER

*Oh Father you know us so well. You know the pain that is bleeding its way through our heads and hearts. You know the panic and loneliness that comes about from feeling that there is no one who can or who wants to understand. Help us to uncurl from our dark corner and turn to you. Help us to tell you all the little things that she or he said, or didn't say. Help us to look at you so we can see your tears.*

---

BRF's Lent books for 1997, *Searching for Truth* by John Polkinghorne and *The Apple of His Eye* by Bridget Plass are available from your local Christian bookshop or, in case of difficulty, direct from BRF. See order form on page 159.

# The Immanence of God

## John Fenton

**T**he first-century Jewish historian Josephus tells us that the robes that the High Priest had to wear at the great festivals in the temple in Jerusalem were kept by the Romans in the Tower of Antonia.

The dates of the festivals were fixed according to the sighting of the new moon, and the vestments had to be taken to the High Priest a week before the holy day to ensure that they were ritually clean: so presumably someone had to go from the High Priest's house to the Antonia to collect the robes, or at least to remind the Romans that they were needed.

The High Priest could not perform his duties without the appropriate vestments.

Which things (one might say) are an allegory. For us, it is not a long blue robe with bells and pomegranates that we need, but our real, true self, free from selfishness and fear, envy and all artificiality. It is not kept in a stone tower in Jerusalem, but with God.

We have to go to him, to get what we need, if we are ever to do his will. Not one, nor even three or four times a year (as with the Jewish festivals and the Day of Atonement) but more frequently than that— every day, every moment.

There is an experience that everybody knows: Something has got into me; I am not myself today. In order to do certain complicated actions—in sport, or in the theatre, or in society—one has first to become inwardly aware of what one is going to do: the gymnast stands waiting on the edge of the mat; the actor in the dressing-room gets into the part; the speaker waits for the cue, collecting the whole matter together before beginning to speak.

Being ourselves and doing what has to be done are not with us automatically and all the time. We have to fetch our real self from somewhere else. Without it, we cannot do the thing properly, whatever it is.

The writers of the New Testament knew this, too, and described it in terms of what you wear. They wrote about putting off the old nature, and putting on Christ, or the armour of God, or faith and love and hope. Your life, Paul said to the Colossians, is hidden from you; it is with Christ, in God (3:2).

We cannot do what we believe

we should do, unless we can collect what we need to do it with; we cannot be ourselves, because our self is not permanently and automatically at our disposal. We cannot assume that we have it by us; it must be fetched; and that takes time.

The 'me' that I need is, in one sense, not me at all. Certainly this was Paul's experience; It is no longer I who live, but it is Christ who lives in me (Galatians 2:20).

It would be a mistake to take this for granted, and live as though I did not need to remember it, and do it. Some things one need not usually remember: to keep on breathing, for example; to sleep and rise, night and day.

But collecting ourselves is not like that; it requires the deliberate and conscious act of asking, going out, fetching, putting on, adjusting, checking to see that it is the right way round.

The New Testament writers say the same thing in another way, too. They and their first readers saw themselves as containers that needed to be filled, or rather, that needed to be emptied first, and then filled. You might be full of wickedness, of the evil forces that they called unclean spirits, demons, Beelzebul. What you needed was to be filled with goodness, kindness, Christ, the Spirit, God.

What we are is always potential, something to be developed, not yet attained, not yet what it should be and shall be.

God is the fulness, with which he will complete all his creatures. We have hardly any idea what this will mean for the other things he made, but we have an inkling how it will be for us; we can just about imagine what it might be like to be filled with God.

To get there, there will have to be two elements: one negative, the other positive. The destruction of the false self, and the receiving of the true self. They are like Babylon and Jerusalem in the Revelation. Dying and rising. Emptying out and being filled. Taking off one set of clothes and putting on another. Turning away and turning towards.

Of course what is to be received and longed for and accepted is infinitely better than what is to be abandoned—the familiar, unattractive me.

What we are on the way towards is God himself, fulfilling us, as he will fulfil everything that he has made. He will be everything, to every body; all, in all.

**John Fenton** *was formerly Principal of St Chad's College, Durham and a Canon of Christ Church in Oxford. He is the author of* The Matthew Passion, *published by BRF, which is available from your local Christian bookshop or, in case of difficulty, direct from BRF. See order form, page 159.*

## 2 Corinthians 1:1–7 (NIrV)

# *Tender love which comforts*

I, Paul, am writing this letter. I am an apostle of Christ Jesus just as God planned. Timothy our brother joins me in writing. Give praise to the God and Father of our Lord Jesus Christ! He is the Father who gives tender love. All comfort comes from him. If we are having trouble, it is so that you will be comforted and renewed. If we are comforted, it is so that you will be comforted. Then you will be able to put up with the same suffering we have gone through. Our hope for you remains firm. We know that you suffer just as we do. In the same way, God comforts you just as he comforts us.

Paul had a problem—and so have we. His problem was how to put things right in his relationship with the Christians in Corinth, with whom he had pastorally been very tough. Our problem is that we don't know what it was that he had been tough with them about.

But that doesn't really matter and it isn't important. It would be interesting to know what the problem was—just as it would interesting to know just what Paul's thorn in the flesh had been. What matters to us, and what is important, is to know what Paul did.

As we see how he acted in his situation it can help us in ours. So far as his thorn in the flesh went he accepted it—along with the fact that it made him weak. But then he gloried in his weakness—and in the discovery he made that he could say 'When I am weak, I am strong' (2 Corinthians 12:10 NIrV).

So far as Paul's pastoral problem with the Corinthian Christians went, he pleaded with them and sought to persuade them to accept him again—along with the severe discipline he had imposed on them. We don't know what it was—but he had disciplined them because of his love for them. Discipline is a dirty word in our generation—but it is a vital component in real love.

### A prayer

*Lord God, you love me, and you want me to grow spiritually. So show me where I need to discipline myself in my own life—and show me how to do it.*
*Show me if there are other people whom I need to discipline, and show me how to do that—because I love them and because you do too.*

SB

2 Corinthians 1:23—2:4 (NIrV)

# Weeping for our sins

I call God as my witness. I wanted to spare you. So I didn't return to Corinth. Your faith is not under our control. You stand firm in your own faith. But we work together with you for your joy. So I made up my mind that I would not make another painful visit to you. If I make you sad, who is going to make me glad? Only you, the one I made sad. I wrote what I did for a special reason. When I came, I didn't want to be troubled by those who should make me glad. I was sure that all of you would share my joy. I was very troubled when I wrote to you. My heart was sad. My eyes were full of tears. I didn't want to make you sad. I wanted to let you know that I love you very deeply.

If we know what it is to weep over someone's sin then it's almost certainly all right to confront them with it. Self-righteous condemnation of another sinner is horrible—and if we are to dare to say anything at all it must be with St Paul as our model. Telling them that they were sinners and telling them that he loved them almost in the same breath. We talk about 'speaking the truth in love'—but our actions and our attitudes don't always match up with our words. Paul's always did—and I suspect that 'speaking the truth in tears' is the acid test of whether we should speak or remain silent.

If we aren't in the habit of weeping, then an alternative test is the fact that we have a very heavy heart: a heart that is deeply troubled by the sin, and deeply troubled at having to speak out and confront it. What also has to be in us is an awareness of our own frailty

and the truth that 'There but for the grace of God go I.' Given all that, and given that we are in a relationship with the person that makes it appropriate, then speak we must. The Apostle Paul had a deep love for the sinners—and a deep hatred for their sin.

## To think about

*Spend a little while reflecting on the reasons why God hates sin. Consider its effect on other people. The suffering caused by violence, injustice, adultery, lying, bad temper...*

SB

FRIDAY 3 JANUARY

## 2 Corinthians 2:12–17 (NIrV)

# *The perfume of life*

I went to Troas to preach the good news about Christ. There I found that the Lord had opened a door of opportunity for me. But I still had no peace of mind. I couldn't find my brother Titus there. So I said good-by to the believers at Troas and went on to Macedonia. Give thanks to God! He always leads us in the winners' parade because we belong to Christ. Through us, God spreads the knowledge of Christ everywhere like perfume. God considers us to be the sweet smell that Christ is spreading among people who are being saved and people who are dying. To the one, we are the smell of death. To the other, we are the perfume of life. Who is able to do that work? Unlike many people, we aren't selling God's word to make money. In fact, it is just the opposite. Because of Christ we speak honestly before God. We speak like people God has sent.

Today when I got off the Oxford bus at Victoria the hot, polluted air smelt of exhaust fumes from the endless stream of cars, buses and lorries. But then, all of a sudden, as I started to walk across to the rail station, there was the sweet, clean smell of new-cut grass. The City of Westminster mowers had been at work on the little triangular garden between three busy roads—and the smell of the new-cut grass made me far more aware of the foulness of the petrol fumes.

For Paul, the knowledge of God was like a beautiful smell—and the people who scented the air with it were Christians. Those who were being drawn and attracted to God loved the smell. But others hated it. Those who loved the smell were being drawn into eternal life—which is the love relationship with God which he created us to enjoy for ever. The people who hated the smell were perishing. Refusing to respond to the love of God. Refusing forgiveness. Refusing life.

### A reflection

*Spend some time thinking about Paul's words, that through him God spread the knowledge of Christ everywhere, like perfume. Spend a few moments thinking about yourself—and the sweet smell that your knowledge of God might be spreading among the people you know. Then pray.*

*SB*

33

### 2 Corinthians 3:1–6 (NIrV)

# *Love letters*

Are we beginning to praise ourselves again? Some people need letters that speak well of them. Do we need those kinds of letters, either to you or from you? You ourselves are our letter. You are written on our hearts. Everyone knows you and reads you. You make it clear that you are a letter from Christ. You are the result of our work for God. You are a letter written not with ink but with the Spirit of the living God. You are a letter written not on tablets made out of stone but on human hearts. Through Christ, we can be sure of this because of our faith in God's power. In ourselves we are not able to claim anything for ourselves. The power to do what we do comes from God. He has given us the power to serve under a new covenant. The covenant is not based on the written Law of Moses. It comes from the Holy Spirit.

'Love letters straight from my heart' is the first line of an old popular song, and the letters that Paul is writing about are really love letters. He has got a good metaphor, and he uses it in two ways.

These Corinthian Christians whom he loves so much (and whom because of his love he disciplined so severely) are a letter written on his heart (by Christ) for him to read—and they are also letters written by the living God for other people to read. They are love letters, because the Spirit of the living God sheds abroad in our hearts the love which God has for us.

'We love [God] because he first loved us,' says 1 John 3:19; it goes on to say that the test of our love for God is that it spills over in love for other people. We love them with the over-flow and the overspill of the love that is poured into our hearts when we are loved. When we know that we are loved, and are ourselves loving in response, then it shows. People can see it in our faces—and as we look at them they will see something of the love of God for them in our eyes, as well as our love for them.

## To think about

*Since you are a letter from the living, loving God to all the people living around you, what are they reading?*

*SB*

### Romans 8:11–17 (RSV)

# Sacrament of the Presence

If the Spirit of him who raised Jesus from the dead dwells in you, he who raised Christ Jesus from the dead will give life to your mortal bodies also through his Spirit which dwells in you... When we cry, 'Abba! Father!' it is the Spirit himself bearing witness with our spirit that we are children of God, and if children, then heirs, heirs of God and fellow heirs with Christ, provided we suffer with him in order that we may also be glorified with him.

If we find it hard to believe that the Spirit really does dwell in us, the sacrament of Holy Communion can help us. 'Do you really live within me, Lord?' we can ask, and an answer can come in the bread and the wine. 'Take, eat, this is my body... This is my blood...' The sacrament can reassure us. The bread and wine are within us—the outward and visible sign of an inward, invisible grace—the sign of the body and blood of Christ within us. And because God is One the Spirit is within us.

All of us who are Christians have the Holy Spirit living within us—but not all of us know it. Sometimes the teaching we are given is defective. Sometimes we just don't want to know—so we grieve the Spirit and act as if our bodies were not the temple of the Holy Spirit.

The Spirit of Christ who is in us will lead us along the way of holiness. He won't lead us by the nose—tugging at us as if we were bulls with a ring in our nose. And he won't drag us by the neck as if we were disobedient dogs. Psalm 32 says the same thing but with different animals: 'Do not be like the horse or the mule, which have no understanding, but must be controlled by bit or bridle' (32:9). We do have understanding, so we are to use it.

We are to listen to the word of God telling us that we are the sons and daughters of God—and to be aware that when we cry out to him and call him Abba, the Spirit of God within us is telling us what is true: 'You are my son.' 'You are my daughter.' 'You are my child.' We can pray to the Father to make us more and more certain of this—with ever increasing conviction and delight through all the days of our life here on earth.

SB

2 Corinthians 3:10–18 (NIrV) (cut)

# The glory of God

The glory of the old covenant is nothing compared with the far greater glory of the new. The glory of the old is fading away. How much greater is the glory of the new! It will last for ever. Since we have that kind of hope, we are very bold. We are not like Moses. He used to cover his face with a veil. That was to keep the people of Israel from looking at his face while the brightness was fading away. But their minds were made stubborn. To this very day, the same veil remains when the old covenant is read... To this very day, when the Law of Moses is read, a veil covers the minds of those who hear it. But when anyone turns to the Lord, the veil is taken away. Now the Lord is the Holy Spirit. And where the Spirit of the Lord is freedom is also there.

Our faces are not covered with a veil. We all display the Lord's glory. We are being changed to become more like him so that we have more and more glory. And the glory comes from the Lord, who is the Holy Spirit.

Paul was a Jew, and he minded passionately that the whole of his beloved race hadn't seen what he had seen—the glory of God in the face of Jesus Christ. But although he is saying that the people of Israel are stubborn and blind he still loves them and yearns for them to turn to Christ. That their minds were 'made stubborn', is as if in some mysterious way it is God himself who has put the veil over their eyes. In Romans he says that it will stay there 'until the full number of the Gentiles has come in.' (11:25, 26)

But what is the glory that we Christians can see and that we all dis-

play? In the Bible the glory of any person or any thing is the person's (or the thing's) true nature shining out like light. 'There is one glory of the sun, and another glory of the moon, and another glory of the stars' (1 Corinthians 15:41)—and the shekinah glory is the shining out of the presence of God. Astonishingly, that is the glory that shines out of us. Only a little shining to start with—but the shining gets brighter.

### A command

*Shine as a light in the world, to the glory of God the Father.*

Baptism service, ASB

SB

2 Corinthians 4:1–7 (NIrV) (cut)

# *The shining of God*

Suppose our good news is covered with a veil. Then it is veiled to those who are dying. The god of this world has blinded the minds of those who don't believe. They can't see the light of the good news of Christ's glory. He is the likeness of God. We do not preach about ourselves. We preach about Jesus Christ. We say that he is Lord. And we serve you because of him. God said, 'Let light shine out of darkness.' (Genesis 1:3) He made his light shine in our hearts. It shows us the light of God's glory in the face of Christ. Treasure is kept in clay jars. In the same way, we have the treasure of the good news in these earthly bodies of ours. That shows that the mighty power of the good news comes from God. It doesn't come from us.

Paul is still writing about people who have been blinded. But in today's reading the one who prevents people from seeing is different. Commentators say that to write 'their minds were made stubborn' indicates that it is God who has made them so—and in our Bible passage yesterday Paul was referring to God's own chosen people, the Jews. But here it is 'the god of this world' who has done the blinding and the veiling.

'Can't you see?' we sometimes say when we are trying to explain something to a person who isn't comprehending—and that is the situation of the people whom Paul is writing about. 'They can't see the light of the good news of Christ's glory,' writes Paul—and 'they' are the people he was preaching to. He had been sent by God to preach to the Gentiles (everyone who wasn't a Jew)—and he appealed to them to choose what was true and right.

Each person must make a personal choice—yet the one who heals their blindness is God, who shines like a light into their darkness. We aren't puppets. We can make real choices, and on the last day we shan't be able to blame God for failing to enlighten us and for not drawing us with his love. He has given us the power to choose. To choose life. Or to choose death.

### Consider

*I have set before you life and death, blessings and curses. Choose life so that you and your descendants may live, loving the Lord your God, obeying him, and holding fast to him; for that means life to you...*

Deuteronomy 30:19–20

*SB*

### 2 Corinthians 4:13–18 (NIrV)

# The weight of glory

We know that God raised the Lord Jesus from the dead. And he will also raise us up with Jesus. He will bring us with you to God in heaven. All of that is for your benefit. God's grace is reaching more and more people. So they will become more and more thankful. They will give glory to God. We don't give up. Our bodies are becoming weaker and weaker. But our spirits are being renewed day by day. Our troubles are small. They last only for a short time. But they are earning for us a glory that will last forever. It is greater than all our troubles.

Death isn't the end of everything for the Christian. It is a door to a life of glory that will last for ever. We know that and believe it because the death of Christ on the cross wasn't the end of everything for him. He died—and his body was put in a tomb. But God raised him from the dead, and the tomb was left empty.

Paul believed that passionately—and he spent his life preaching about it. The good news is that through the death of Christ our sins are forgiven and we have eternal life. A life lived in a relationship of love with the God who created us to be loved and to love. Eternal life which begins on this side of the grave and continues on the other side of death.

But on the other side we shan't be disembodied spirits. We shall have bodies. Spiritual bodies, it says, but bodies (and tomorrow we shall look at what Paul says about 'our house in heaven' which is our resurrection body).

Paul's human body was getting weaker. Partly through the sufferings and persecutions of his ministry as an apostle. And presumably partly because he was simply getting older. It happens to all of us. But the wonderful thing is that as our bodies get frailer our spirits can get stronger.

The RSV translation of verses 16–21, is a wonderful passage to meditate on.

## Meditate

*So we do not lose heart. Though our outer nature is wasting away, our inner nature is being renewed every day. For this slight momentary affliction is preparing for us an eternal weight of glory beyond all comparison, because we look not to the things that are seen but to the things that are unseen; for the things that are seen are transient, but the things that are unseen are eternal.*

SB

## 2 Corinthians 5:1–10 (NIrV) (cut)

# *A house in heaven*

We know that the earthly tent we live in will be destroyed. But we have a building made by God. It is a house in heaven that lasts for ever. Human hands did not build it... While we live in this tent of ours, we groan under our heavy load. We don't want to be naked. We want to be dressed with our house in heaven. What must die will be swallowed up by life. God has made us for that very purpose. He has given us the Holy Spirit as a down payment. The Spirit makes us sure of what is still to come. So here is what we can always be certain about. As long as we are at home in our bodies. we are away from the Lord. We live by believing, not by seeing. We are certain about that.

Life was tough for Paul and for those early believers—and often it's tough for us. It's a beautiful world that we live in, and 'The earth is filled with the grandeur of God' (Gerard Manley Hopkins). God has 'given us all things richly to enjoy'—and we can know an astonishing joy that comes to us from God.

But there is a dark and a suffering side to life and to the world that we live in—and our human bodies aren't going to live for ever.

Yesterday at his funeral I watched the curtains drawn round Douglas Cleverley Ford's coffin—and his body went to be cremated. But for him, as for Paul, that isn't the end of the matter. Douglas' body was getting frail—and he was getting weary. And the earthly tent he lived in has been destroyed now. While he lived in it he groaned—although he loved people

and he loved his garden and the created world.

But Paul says that after we die we shall live in something far more permanent than a tent: 'a building made by God... a house in heaven that lasts for ever'.

We shan't be naked spirits—ghost-like and unsubstantial. We shall (to use a different picture) be dressed—in the new clothes of our resurrection body. Clothes that will be a perfect fit for us—so that our new bodies perfectly express the person that is us.

### A prayer

*Thank you, Lord God, for the house in heaven that you are building for me. Thank you that it will last for ever, and that I shall be with you for ever. Amen.*
            *SB*

### 2 Corinthians 5:17–21 (NIrV)

# *All things new*

Anyone who believes in Christ is a new creation. The old is gone! The new has come! It is all from God. He has brought us back to himself through Christ's death on the cross. And he has given us the task of bringing others back to him through Christ. God was bringing the world back to himself through Christ. He did not hold people's sins against them. God has trusted us with the message that people may be brought back to him. So we are Christ's official messengers. It is as if God were making his appeal through us. Here is what Christ wants us to beg you to do. Come back to God! Christ didn't have any sin. But God made him become sin for us. So we can be made right with God because of what Christ has done for us.

Paul has been likening the creation of the Christian to the creation of the world. Before the galaxies and the worlds came into being, God spoke a word into the darkness: 'Let there be light.'

Before the Christian comes into being God speaks a word into the darkness of the human heart: 'Let there be light.'

There isn't space in this small note to discuss God's call and our response (or lack of it) in the making of the new creation. But Paul says that if we believe then this is what we are: 'a new creation. The old is gone! The new has come!'

What has gone is our alienation from God and our wrong fear of him. There is a right fear: the holy awe and dread which is the beginning of the wisdom. The wrong fear is like Adam's

in the story of Eden: 'I was afraid, and so I hid myself.' The story says that God was calling Adam's name in the garden—and Paul says that he is still calling to us. Through Paul, then the apostles—and, through the years, through all those who preach the Gospel and share the message: 'Come back to God.'

Christ died for us to bring us back—and on the cross the sinless one was 'made sin' for us.

### Reflect

*Do I realize that I am 'a new creation'—with a new life, a new relationship with God, and a new purpose?*

SB

2 Corinthians 7:8–13 (NIrV)

# Love that confronts

Even if my letter made you sad, I'm not sorry I sent it. At first I was sorry. I see that my letter hurt you, but only for a little while. Now I am happy. I'm not happy because you were made sad. I'm happy because your sadness led you to turn away from your sins... Godly sadness causes us to turn away from our sins and be saved. And we are certainly not sorry about that! But worldly sadness brings death. Look at what that godly sadness has produced in you. You are working hard to clear yourselves. You are angry and alarmed. You are longing to see me. You are concerned. You are ready to make sure that the right thing is done. In every way you have proved that you are not guilty in that matter.

Paul's letter had upset them, but it had done what he wanted it to do. We don't know what that was—because we don't know what the original offence had been. But his actions can give us a model for our own if we are in similar situation.

He confronted them with their wrongdoing—and we saw earlier that he did it with tears in his eyes and with love in his heart.

He gave them time to think things over—and didn't go to see them while they were working things out.

We can't *make* people act in the right way. That's their decision. But we can confront them if they are doing something wrong—and the New Testament tells us that we should: 'If your brother sins against you, go to him and show him his fault. But do it privately, just between yourselves. If he listens to you, you have won your brother back. But if he will not listen to you, take one or two other persons with you, so that "every accusation may be upheld by the testimony of two or more witnesses," as the scripture says. And if he will not listen to them, then tell the whole thing to the church. Finally, if he will not listen to the church, treat him as though he were a pagan or a tax collector' (Matthew 18:15–17, GNB).

A prayer before you confront someone

*Father, out of your great love for that person, convict them of their sin—and give me the wisdom and the courage to say what needs to be said. Amen.*

SB

## Isaiah 49:5–6 (NRSV)

# *I am the light of the world*

And now the Lord says, who formed me in the womb to be his servant, to bring Jacob back to him, and that Israel might be gathered to him, for I am honoured in the sight of the Lord, and my God has become my strength—he says, 'It is too light a thing that you should be my servant to raise up the tribes of Jacob and to restore the survivors of Israel; I will give you as a light to the nations, that my salvation may reach to the end of the earth.'

'Can light and darkness be friends?' Paul wrote in the passage from 2 Corinthians which we shall read tomorrow, expecting the answer, 'No'—and he was writing to deter a Christian believer from marrying an unbeliever.

Light in the Bible represents the presence of God, and the spiritual wisdom and enlightenment that only God can give. It is impossible for light to co-exist with the presence of darkness because the moment the light enters in the darkness is banished.

In physical terms darkness has no real existence. Light consists of particles (which behave like waves). Darkness is the absence of light. 'Light has come into the world,' it says in the Gospel of John, 'but men loved darkness instead of light because their deeds were evil. Everyone who does evil hates the light, and will not come to the light for fear that his deeds will be exposed. But whoever lives by the truth comes into the light, so that it may be plainly seen that what he has done has been done through God' (John 3:19–21, NIV).

Today is the first Sunday after Epiphany, and 'epiphany' means manifestation. To manifest means to 'show plainly to eye or mind; be evidence of, prove'; and the epiphany of Christ is the revelation of God. 'He who has seen me has seen the Father.'(John 14:9)

God is like Jesus—and he wants the whole world to know that.

### A prayer

*Eternal God, who by the shining of a star led the wise men to the worship of your Son; guide by his light the nations of the earth, that the whole world may behold your glory; through Jesus Christ our Lord.*

The Collect for Epiphany, ASB

SB

### 2 Corinthians 6:14–16 (NIrV)

# Light and darkness

Do not be joined to unbelievers. What do right and wrong have in common? Can light and darkness be friends? How can Christ and Satan agree? What does a believer have in common with an unbeliever? How can the temple of the true God and the statues of other gods agree? We are the temple of the living God.

These are strong words that Paul is using. Intolerant and unaccepting. The Western world finds *Alice in Wonderland* far more to their taste than St Paul: 'Everyone has won,' said the Dodo. 'Everyone must have prizes.' But what if they haven't won? What if they haven't even started in the race (and Paul likens the Christian life to a race). What if they've got things wrong and if their beliefs about God are seriously defective? Because if Christians have got it right then, to the extent that they differ, the other religions are wrong.

God is like Jesus, and his nature and his name is love. He loves sinners but he hates their sin; he is quite specific about what sin is. He suffers for us and with us—and he is present in all places and in all things. Yet he is wholly other than them. In Christ 'all things hold together' (Colossians 1:17) and he 'upholds all things by his word of power' (Hebrews 1:3).

Yet there is a special indwelling in the Christian of the One who upholds and is present in all things and in all people, because the Christian worships him and knows who he is. So Christians are the temple of the Holy Spirit. That is true of the individual Christian and of the whole people of God who are the body of Christ. Those who praise God through Jesus Christ their Lord.

And you can't join *that* person, says Paul, to someone who isn't like that. The someone who isn't like that is beloved by God and created by God. 'God… the Saviour of all men, and especially of those who believe' (1 Timothy 4:10). But the someone who doesn't know God is not the temple of the Holy Spirit, because that special, intimate relationship does not exist. The Holy Spirit of God is not worshipped or honoured by them—and the one is as different from the other as light is from darkness.

A prayer

*Lord Jesus Christ, you are the light of the world. Help me to see the difference between light and darkness, and between right and wrong. Amen.*

SB

2 Corinthians 8:1–12 (NIrV) (cut)

# *Love that gives*

Brothers and sisters, we want you to know about the grace that God has given to the churches in Macedonia. They have suffered a great deal. But their joy was more than full. Even though they were very poor, they gave very freely... First they gave themselves to the Lord. Then they gave themselves to us in keeping with what the Lord wanted... You do well in everything else. You do well in faith and in speaking. You do well in knowledge and in complete commitment. And you do well in your love for us. So make sure that you also do well in the grace of giving to others... You know the grace shown by our Lord Jesus Christ. Even though he was rich, he became poor to help you. Because he became poor, you can become rich.

The self-giving love of God is at the heart of creation and of redemption. God created the world out of his love and redeemed it for the same reason. 'God so loved the world that he gave...' (John 3:16).

Sometimes at the start of a Christian life the new believer can be so aware of the wonder of the self-giving love of God that there is an overspill of love to everyone and everything around them. 'We love because he first loved us,' it says in 1 John 4:19—and as we delight in being loved we shall grow in love. Love for God and love for people.

At some stage in our Christian life we shall realize that giving our love will also mean (when it is necessary and needed) giving our money. 'I am not commanding you to do it' Paul wrote, 'But I want to put you to the test. I want to find out if you really love God.' (verse 8:8 in the middle of today's passage).

Paul taught his converts about the joy and the privilege of giving. But they needed to get the order right—and so do we. First they had to give themselves to God—and so do we. Then to Paul—and our equivalent would be our personal commitment in love to those who have ministered the faith to us. Then—and only then—they gave their money, because that is what they deeply wanted to do.

### A prayer

*Lord God, thank you for all that you have given to me. Help me to give to other people. To give my love—and to give my money.*

SB

2 Corinthians 9:6–11 (NIrV) (cut)

# Such lavish giving

The one who plants only a little will gather only a little. And the one who plants a lot will gather a lot. You should each give what you have decided in your heart to give. You shouldn't give if you don't want to. You shouldn't give because you are forced to. God loves a cheerful giver. And God is able to shower all kinds of blessings on you. In all things and at all times you will have everything you need... God supplies seed to the planter. He supplies bread for food. God will also supply and increase the amount of your seed. He will increase the results of your good works. You will be made rich in every way. Then you can always give freely. We will take your many gifts to the people who need them. And they will give thanks to God.

This year I bought a small packet of nicotiana—the tobacco plant with a wonderful smell and flowers ranging from white through pale pink to deep crimson. In that tiny packet there were two thousand seeds. A friend is growing them for her garden and for mine, and there will be plenty to give away to other people as well.

We are made in the image and likeness of God, who is a lavish and profuse giver and creator. Billions of stars. Millions of people. And thousands of species of created things, plants, fish, birds and animals.

Two thousand nicotiana seeds in one small packet. So many seeds in the world and stars in the sky that no one can count them. And it is with that knowledge—and with the Spirit of that God within us—that we are to give. Lavishly and generously. Joyfully.

And with great delight.

We shan't run short ourselves—and we shall get a rich dividend and an abundant harvest. Though that's not to be the motive for our giving. Our giving is to come from our heart, simply because we love.

### A prayer

*Creator God, I praise you for the abundance of your creation. For the stars and the galaxies. For our world and all that is in it. So many wonderful and beautiful species—trees and plants, fishes and birds, insects and animals. And human beings made in your imge and likeness. Help us to live and to love like you. To live life more abundantly and to give more abundantly. Amen.*

SB

2 Corinthians 11:21–31 (NIrV) (cut)

# *The authority of love*

What anyone else dares to brag about, I also dare to brag about. I'm speaking like a fool. Are they Hebrews? So am I... Are they Abraham's children? So am I. Are they serving Christ? I am serving him even more... I have worked much harder. I have been in prison more often. I have suffered terrible beatings. Again and again I almost died... I have been in danger from people from my own country. I have been in danger from those who aren't Jews. I have been in danger in the city, in the country, and at sea... I have worked very hard. Often I have gone without sleep. I have been hungry and thirsty. Often I have gone without food. I have been cold and naked. Besides everything else, every day I am concerned about all the churches. It is a very heavy load. If anyone is weak, I feel weak. If anyone is led into sin, I burn on the inside. If I have to brag, I will brag about the things that show how weak I am.

It seems a strange way for an apostle to go on. To brag and to boast. But he is in the business of convincing them that he really is an apostle—and that he therefore really does have authority over them.

But it's not the authority of a dictator or a despot. It's the authority of love, given to him by Christ. And when Christ told *his* disciples that 'All authority in heaven and earth has been given to me', the next thing he did was to take a towel and a bowl of water and wash their feet—the dirty job that no one else wanted to do.

That was the model for Paul's apostleship—and he had lived it out and almost died in the process. He's telling them all these things to show them that he's got it right—and that the 'super-apostles' who had led them into error were wrong. 'People like that are false apostles,' he wrote. 'They work hard to trick others. They only pretend to be apostles of Christ. That comes as no surprise. Even Satan himself pretends to be an angel of light. So it doesn't surprise us that those who serve Satan pretend to be serving God. They will finally get exactly what they should.' (11:13–15).

A prayer

*Lord Jesus, help me to recognize real authority.*

SB

2 Corinthians 12:1–10 (NIrV) (cut)

# Weak and strong

I want to talk about what the Lord has shown me. I know a believer in Christ who was taken up to the third heaven fourteen years ago... I don't know if that man was in his body or out of it. Only God knows... But I do know that he was taken up to paradise. He heard things that couldn't be put into words. They were things that people aren't allowed to talk about. I could have become proud of myself because of the amazing and wonderful things God has shown me. So I was given a problem that caused pain in my body. It is a messenger from Satan to make me suffer. Three times I begged the Lord to take it away from me. But he said to me, 'My grace is all you need. My power is strongest when you are weak.' So I am very happy to brag about how weak I am. Then Christ's power can rest on me... When I am weak, I am strong.

Paul is still bragging and boasting, but only because they need to know the truth. He never gives us the details we'd probably like to know—either about his spiritul experience or his thorn in the flesh. But here again his actions can be the model for ours.

• Virtual silence about his own trouble. He didn't write about it or talk about it. What he did talk about was the good news of the gospel and the glory of God.

• Total acceptance of his painful problem—after praying to the Lord about it and getting the answer 'no' to his request.

We can do the same with the things that cause us pain. It might be the circumstances of our life. Perhaps an unhappy or a disappointing marriage—or no marriage at all when we would have preferred it otherwise. Perhaps an illness that doesn't respond to the prayer for healing.

There is a deep heart-peace in acceptance—and in the pain, the weakness and the disappointment the power of Christ can rest on us, as it did on Paul.

### A prayer

*O God, grant us the serenity to accept what cannot be changed, the courage to change what can be changed, and the wisdom to know the difference.*

Reinhold Niebuhr

SB

**2 Corinthians 13:5–10 & 11–14 (NIrV)**

# *Tests of belief*

Take a good look at yourselves to see if you are really believers.
Test yourselves. Don't you realize that Christ Jesus is in you?
Unless, of course, you fail the test!

When Paul told these Christians to test themselves to see if they really were believers he must have thought they would know how to do it. Our generation of Christians wouldn't be so sure. 'I *hope* I'm a Christian' people say—but they are very uncertain about it. But the New Testament says that we can know and gives us ways to test ourselves. The following all come from 1 John.

The test of obedience. 'Now by this we may be sure that we know him, if we obey his commandments' (2:3). We don't keep them perfectly, but a true believer will never disobey them flagrantly.

The test of knowing I am a sinner. The writers of the New Testament knew that Christians are still sinners. But we are sinners who have been and are continually being forgiven. 'If we say that we have no sin, we deceive ourselves, and the truth is not in us. If we confess our sins, he who is faithful will forgive us our sins and cleanse us from all unrighteousness' (1:8,9).

The test of love. 'We know that we have passed from death to life because we love one another. Whoever does not love abides in death' (3:14).

The test of belief. 'And this is his commandment, that we should believe in the name of his Son Jesus Christ and love one another, just as he has commanded us. All who obey his commandments abide in him, and he abides in them. And by this we know that he abides in us, by the Spirit that he has given us' (3:23–24).

### Reflect

*Finally, brothers and sisters, goodbye. Try to be perfect. Pay attention to what I'm saying. Agree with one another. Live in peace. And the God who gives love and peace will be with you... May the grace shown by the Lord Jesus Christ, and the love that God has given us, and the sharing of life brought about by the Holy Spirit be with you all.*

(vv.11–14)

*SB*

# *The Song of Solomon*

The Song of Solomon is considered by Orientals to be eminently chaste, honouring marriage and the joys of wedded life. It can also be read with great profit as an allegory of Christ's love for the church, but do just enjoy it as a poem as well. Settle down and read the whole thing through from beginning to end without worrying too much about what its exact meaning might be. My reflections are, as usual, suggestive of one who has been ambushed rather than instructed by scripture.

*Adrian Plass*

Editor's note:

The Bible readings from 2 Corinthians are taken from a new version of the NIV. Published by Hodder and Stoughton, the New International Reader's Version (NIrV) is intended to be an 'easy read'.

I think there is real beauty and poetry in this simplified version, with its short, poignant sentences. The sheer shortness of them makes it very hard to miss the point.

I thought that *New Daylight* readers might enjoy it, as I have done. So we asked Hodder and Stoughton to give us permission to use it. This they have generously done, and we are very grateful.

*Shelagh Brown*

### Song of Solomon 1:1–4 (NIV)

# *The power and the perfume*

Solomon's Song of Songs. Let him kiss me with the kisses of his mouth—for your love is more delightful than wine. Pleasing is the fragrance of your perfumes; your name is like perfume poured out. No wonder the maidens love you! Take me away with you—let us hurry! Let the king bring me into his chambers. We rejoice and delight in you; we will praise your love more than wine. How right they are to adore you!

It's refreshing to plunge into an atmosphere as rich with the ecstasy of lovers as the Song of Solomon. I pray you will feel closer to the heart of God, and more safely held by the divine intelligence than ever, as you read this passionate allegory of spiritual desire and union. There is something reassuring about God electing to use such a human scenario in which to reveal his feelings for us.

One line in this early passage, though, the one about the lover's name being like perfume poured out, makes me rather sad. Don't misunderstand me, I love the idea. It reminds me of visits to our home by special friends and family members. When one of my children calls out that one of these favourite people is at the door, the very mention of the name seems to add a new and sweeter scent to the day. I felt the same thing even more pungently as a child. One of my brothers would yell, 'Mum's back!', and suddenly everything was—well—all right again. The house was warm and normal and scented with safety.

My sadness is about the name of Jesus. Since becoming a Christian in the mid-sixties that name has had the power to strengthen me, warm me, support me, make me cry, remind me who I belong to and what I should be doing, or a combination of those things. For some, however, the word 'Jesus' triggers feelings of something very close to disgust and repulsion, largely because the man who bore that name has been relentlessly presented by far too many of those who claim to follow him, as a passionless and really rather pathetic personality, who bleats thinly and unattractively about the need for people to stop doing bad things. How sad.

The Song of Solomon tips the balance way over in the other direction, without one jot of moral or spiritual compromise, and the sweet scent of the name of Jesus is on every page.

Prayer

*Restore the power and perfume of your name, Lord.*

AP

## Song of Solomon 1:5–6 (NIV)

# The place where we are

Dark am I, yet lovely, O daughters of Jerusalem, dark like the tents of Kedar, like the tent curtains of Solomon. Do not stare at me because I am dark, because I am darkened by the sun. My mother's sons were angry with me and made me take care of the vineyards; my own vineyard I have neglected.

Some aspects of this poem are very difficult to understand, but it appears that the girl in this passage has been sent by her brothers to work in their vineyard under the hot sun. As a result she is bronzed and beautiful, and in this state she is later encountered by Solomon (disguised as a shepherd?), who falls in love with her and eventually makes her his bride.

The theme isn't an uncommon one—I suppose Cinderella is more or less the same story in a different form—but, as a picture of Christian experience it has a particular significance, namely, that the Holy Spirit will find us and demonstrate the power of love to us in the place where we are, rather than in the place where we perhaps thought we ought to be. Often, in addition, the face of God appears to us at first in the guise of a person or set of events that are without specifically Christian labels of any kind.

Today, as I look back to the days before I became a Christian, I can see, as I was unable to see then (or for some years after my conversion, to be honest), the ways in which God fathered me in times of desolation. I recall, for instance, a cafe in Tunbridge Wells where, as a lost, bored, broke and singularly unattractive teenager I spent much of my time. The manageress, an Italian lady named Inez, was one of the very few rays of light in an otherwise bleak world. She fed me occasionally, smiled at me, talked to me, made me feel I was not entirely a waste of time. I hope she reads this. I'd love her to know how grateful I was and am. Today, I also thank God for being there for me, in her, at a time when I didn't even know he existed.

If you want to meet Jesus you are not in the wrong place, because that is the place where he will find you, and then you will go to the ball.

### Prayer

*Father, some of us feel that we have been badly treated and have ended up in the wrong place. Visit us with your love, Lord, in the place where we are.*

*AP*

51

## Song of Solomon 1:12–17 (NIV)

# *Forever in love*

While the king was at his table, my perfume spread its fragrance. My lover is to me a sachet of myrrh resting between my breasts. My lover is to me a cluster of henna blossoms from the vineyards of En Gedi. How beautiful you are, my darling! Oh, how beautiful! Your eyes are doves. How handsome you are, my lover! Oh, how charming! And our bed is verdant. The beams of our house are cedars; our rafters are firs.

Being in love is such a total thing, isn't it? This passage has that dreamy, all-absorbed, repetitive quality that one associates with the whole business of falling head over heels in love.

Two friends of ours fell in love when we were living in the Midlands. We knew them both very well, but separately, if you know what I mean. In fact, they probably first met at our house. Philip and Jane were both halfway through their fifties, and we were surprised and a little alarmed on first hearing that a relationship had not only begun, but was rocketing down the road towards marriage! How would these two very distinct and independent personalities cope with sharing personal space at this stage in their lives? I went out for a drink with Philip and asked him how things were going. He was in a state of terminal gooiness. Apparently he and Jane felt exactly the same about absolutely everything.

'Isn't that a remarkable coincidence?' said Philip.

'Yes, Philip,' I confirmed superfluously, 'that's a remarkable coincidence.'

'Do you know,' went on Philip

dreamily, 'I was sitting in this very same pub with Jane the other evening, and she accidentally spilt some of her drink on my trousers.'

'Oh, dear,' I said, 'how annoying that must have—'

'I said to her, "Jane, don't worry, I count it a privilege to have your drink spilt on me—I really do..."'

I didn't listen to any more after that.

Philip and Jane are happily not counting it a privilege to spill drinks all over each other nowadays, and I hope they'll have a very pleasant life together.

Why have I been rambling on about my friends? Well, it interests me to reflect on the fact that the idyllic 'in love-ness' expressed in these verses from Solomon's poem will never actually fade when it comes to our relationship with God. Read it again and reflect on the fact that this dream is for ever.

Prayer

*Help us to never fall out of love with you, Lord.*

AP

Song of Solomon 2:1–3 (NIV)

# *A lily among thorns*

I am a rose of Sharon, a lily of the valleys. Like a lily among thorns is my darling among the maidens. Like an apple tree among the trees of the forest is my lover among the young men. I delight to sit in his shade, and his fruit is sweet to my taste.

This is a beautiful piece of writing, isn't it? No comment of mine can add very much. There is one little thing that strikes me, though. (Yes, yes, you're right—there's always some little thing that strikes me). It's the line where the man compares his love among maidens to a lily among brambles. What does this mean?

Here are two possible interpretations, both of which have interesting implications.

First, there's a suggestion of vulnerability. Brambles are notoriously apt to choke or impede the growth of more tender plants. Perhaps there's a hint here of the risk taken by God in allowing Jesus to be exposed as a real man to the tangles and thorns of unsaved humanity. Certainly, the sight of that baby, fragile and dependent, in the stable in Bethlehem, is one which God and all his angels must have gazed on with great pride and great fear. How would we look after him? What would happen to him in the end? The answer, of course, is that Mary and Joseph seem to have done very well, but, between us all, we crucified him. The lily was crushed but not destroyed.

This principle of the vulnerability of Jesus is, I believe, an important part of our understanding of how the Body of Christ on earth should function today. A later note mentioning Mother Teresa might explain more of what I mean by that.

The second interpretation is simply that something very beautiful and special is growing in the midst of us, however wild and cheap life on News at Ten (and in our living-rooms) may seem sometimes. In each one of us, in the centre of every situation, at the heart of every storm, plague and tragedy, the flowering, or the first shoots, or, at the very least, the seeds of the growth of love can never be destroyed. And, just in case anyone thinks that's soppy talk, let me say, on behalf of myself and many others, that it is the lily among the brambles that has made it possible to survive on many, many occasions.

Prayer

*Jesus, so vulnerable, so beautiful, so strong, help us to stand.*

AP

### Song of Solomon 2: 4–7 (NIV)

# *Ordinary heroes*

He has taken me to the banquet hall, and his banner over me is love. Strengthen me with raisins, refresh me with apples, for I am faint with love. His left arm is under my head, and his right arm embraces me. Daughters of Jerusalem, I charge you by the gazelles and by the does of the field: Do not arouse or awaken love until it so desires.

'Mum! I'm home, Mum, guess what—Robert Wilson's asked me to go round his tonight, an' I'm faint with love. Get the raisins out an' bung us an apple—I need a bit of sustaining...'

Initially it seems difficult to relate the stylized romance of such a distant culture and time to contemporary experience, but, in fact, human beings have been more or less the same throughout history, and especially when it comes to affairs of the heart. Only the context and the details change (although even raisins and apples reappear nowadays as muesli, don't they? Presumably Solomon's lover's mum made sure she had a good nourishing breakfast before going out romancing every morning).

Understanding the relative 'ordinariness' of biblical characters can help to develop a constructive relationship with scripture. For years, presumably influenced by grimly dramatic lithographs in our big family bible, and feature films in which Charlton Heston or Victor Mature gazed at the horizon accompanied by a full orchestra, my vague notion was that people like Moses and Samuel were (a) American (b) fifteen feet tall, and (c) incapable of speaking any sentence that didn't drip with cosmic significance. What rubbish!

God has always dealt with frail human beings because there isn't any other sort about. Some of the great characters of the Old Testament had particular talents and qualities, but, on reading accounts of their lives we discover that they also had pronounced faults and weaknesses. A barrier to personal involvement in passages like today's, and in much of the rest of the Bible, is this illusory feeling that our emotions, experiences, relationships and spiritual battles are somehow puny and unimportant by comparison with the 'heroes' of scripture.

Rest assured; if you've ever been in love, you will understand the Song of Solomon, and if you're serving God in the twentieth century, you are already starring in an epic all of your own.

### Thought

*If the Bible had been written today, in our society, would we have the Book of George, and the Book of Irene, and the Book of Stan, and the Book of...?*

AP

Song of Solomon 2:10–13, 16–17 (NIV)

# A season for all men

My lover spoke and said to me, 'Arise, my darling, my beautiful one, and come with me. See! The winter is past; the rains are over and gone. Flowers appear on the earth; the season of singing has come, the cooing of doves is heard in our land. The fig-tree forms its early fruit; the blossoming vines spread their fragrance. Arise, come, my darling; my beautiful one, come with me.'... My lover is mine and I am his; he browses among the lilies. Until the day breaks and the shadows flee, turn, my lover, and be like a gazelle or like a young stag on the rugged hills.

This must be one of the most famous Springtime rhapsodies of all time, sung by one, not only enraptured by the new season, but also in love, a pretty unbeatable combination.

One of the cliches of Christianity is the spiritual symbolism of the seasons, isn't it? We're born, we live, we pass through the evening of our lives, we die, we are born again. These parallels have only become cliches, of course, because they really do resonate, not just with specifically Christian cycles, but with the very rhythm of living itself. As the years go by my gratitude for seasonal change intensifies. Living through a year in this country is like travelling in majestic slow motion on the most magnificent theme park ride that could ever be devised.

The symbols? Well, for me there are symbols within symbols. Here's an example.

In front of our house stands a large Japanese flowering cherry. The tree has obviously been there for years. For forty-nine weeks of the year, this sturdy growth is undistinguished, but when the spring comes it explodes into a triumph of pink blossom. For three weeks a huge orb of colour shines over the street like the most precious of precious jewels, glowing with particular magnificence under blue skies. After this brief but spectacularly successful run the performance ends, and our neighbours start getting annoyed about soggy blossom all over their front gardens.

When I was ill a decade ago, the blooming of that tree was like a sign from heaven, suggesting to me that God employs a special magic to bring beauty out of dullness. Every year I look forward to a repeat of that little exercise in optimism, a sort of arboreal rainbow, a symbol within a symbol.

I love springtime.

### Prayer

*Thank you for the seasons and the possibility of change.*

AP

### Song of Solomon 3:1–4 (NIV)

# *Lost lovers*

All night long on my bed I looked for the one my heart loves; I looked for him but did not find him. I will get up now and go about the city, through its streets and squares; I will search for the one my heart loves. So I looked for him but did not find him. The watchmen found me as they made their rounds in the city. "Have you seen the one my heart loves?" Scarcely had I passed them when I found the one my heart loves. I held him and would not let him go till I had brought him to my mother's house, to the room of the one who conceived me.

Of all the heart-rending letters that people send me from time to time, the ones that upset me most (perhaps because I can identify with them) are those in which a desperate but unfulfilled desire for God is expressed. Like the speaker in this passage these unhappy souls cry out in the dark night of their desolation for some sign or indication that they are not alone—that God really does hear them and love them, that they will eventually be united with him and that—well, you know—that everything will be warm and fuzzy and wonderful.

Often, these folk have already sought and received most of the statutory varieties of advice, and are hoping I might offer some new, super-effective idea that will transform their lives. Oh, dear!

I suppose if God was a system, or a mechanism, or even a sheet of M.F.I. instructions, I might be able to help in that way, but he isn't—he is a creative, dynamic personality who cannot be adjusted or programmed to produce a particular effect.

When you set against that the complexity of each of the human beings who has dealings with him, the problem appears to become even more insoluble. What I can say, from personal experience, is that if you are one of these lost lovers, a right time will come to rise from your bed and go about the city, in the streets and in the squares, looking for your God, and then you will meet him. But it must be the right time, the moment that he has chosen for you.

When you do find him—and you will—don't take him for granted. Don't let him go.

### Prayer

*Father, hear the cries from the dark and stretch out your arms towards us. We want to be with you so much.*

AP

Song of Solomon 4:1, 5–7 (NIV)

# Too good to be true

How beautiful you are, my darling! Oh, how beautiful! Your eyes behind your veil are doves. Your hair is like a flock of goats descending from Mount Gilead... Your two breasts are like two fawns, like twin fawns of a gazelle that browse among the lilies. Until the day breaks and the shadows flee, I will go to the mountain of myrrh and to the hill of incense. All beautiful you are, my darling; there is no flaw in you.

Some years ago an advert appeared in *The Times*. The small panel on the back page simply offered a free car—a mini—to the first person who replied. There were no strings attached, nothing to be paid, in fact, no catch at all. Someone could have had a car for nothing, but not a single person responded. Presumably readers thought they'd be 'done' in some way. Of course, that was exactly the reaction the advertisers had expected; nevertheless, the car really was there for the taking.

Do you think people were silly to be wary? Well, look at this passage, which offers something rather more valuable than a mini, and ask yourself whether you think it's for real. Let me explain.

The Song of Solomon is many things, but, perhaps most importantly, it is, as I mentioned in the introduction, a picture of God's love for his bride, the church. That, in case you didn't realize it, means you—and me. Now, I'd like us to ask ourselves the following question. Leaving aside items such as having breasts like two

fawns, do we honestly believe that this is what God sees when he looks at us?

Are we—not just beautiful—but very beautiful to him? Does he really think us lovely? Could we possibly be without flaw in his sight? Is it conceivable that we stir such excited pleasure in his breast?

He says this is all true. Perhaps there's a catch. I don't think so. Even less than when the Plass family go fishing. We are so much in the groove of self-criticism that we forget we are caught up with Christ. We are as beautiful as he is, not because of what we are or do, but because he is in us and we are in him. Can we accept that? Come on—we missed out on the mini—let's have a go.

### Prayer

*Some of us don't feel very beautiful, Lord. Help us to get lost in your love.*
                                                    *AP*

Song of Solomon 4:9–11 (NIV)

# Sweet nothings

You have stolen my heart, my sister, my bride; you have stolen my heart with one glance of your eyes, with one jewel of your necklace. How delightful is your love, my sister, my bride! How much more pleasing is your love than wine, and the fragrance of your perfume than any spice! Your lips drop sweetness as the honeycomb, my bride; milk and honey are under your tongue. The fragrance of your garments is like that of Lebanon.

I wish I was a little better at the old sweet nothings. Mind you, my wife would be deeply suspicious if I suddenly nestled up and told her that honey and milk are under her tongue, and the scent of her garments is like the scent of Lebanon. As for claiming that I regard her love as much better than wine—I'm not at all sure she'd believe me.

Seriously, it does seem a pity that many marriages deteriorate, not just into lack of romance, but actual conflict. A dismally common view of marriage is exemplified by a scene I once witnessed in a laundrette. As I entered a loud argument was going on between a man and woman in their early sixties.

'You don't understand listenin', do you?' shouted the lady. 'All you can do is make a noise!'

'Go on, get out of it!' returned the man furiously. 'You're nothin' but a stupid, mouthy old ratbag!'

'Don't worry!' she snapped. 'I don't want to be anywhere you might be!'

And with that, she swept through the door and disappeared.

A pear-shaped lady who'd observed hostilities from beside the drying machines shifted slightly on her seat and addressed the man in dispassionate tones. 'She your wife, then?'

The man stopped muttering and stared at her.

'Married to 'er!' he said incredulously, 'I wouldn't marry 'er if she was the last woman on earth!'

'Oh,' said the pear-shaped lady, dispassionate as ever, 'I thought she must be your wife the way you was talkin' to 'er.'

An extreme example of how marriage is seen, perhaps, but it does seem such a shame that so many marriages begin as romances, only to decline to the point where your marriage partner is the only person you're ever really nasty to.

Prayer

*Lord, we can't reach Solomon's standard, but we'd like to bring some romance back into our marriages. Help those of us who are married to see our partners with fresh eyes, and begin to appreciate them all over again.*

AP

Song of Solomon 4:12–16 (NIV)

# *Unlocking*

You are a garden locked up, my sister, my bride; you are a spring enclosed, a sealed fountain. Your plants are an orchard of pomegranates with choice fruits, with henna and nard, nard and saffron, calamus and cinnamon, with every kind of incense tree, with myrrh and aloes and all the finest spices. You are a garden fountain, a well of flowing water streaming down from Lebanon. Awake, north wind, and come, south wind! Blow on my garden, that its fragrance may spread abroad. Let my lover come into his garden and taste its choice fruits.

I mentioned in an earlier note that I occasionally look back with horror to the time when, as a teenage truant of fifteen or sixteen, I wandered aimlessly around Tunbridge Wells with no money and no prospects. It isn't the idea of the aimless wandering that causes my horror—that has remained one of my favourite hobbies—it's the memory of how I dealt with feelings of gross inadequacy about most of my relationships. I developed a habit of scathing sarcasm that probably alienated more people than I ever imagined at the time. Lowest form of wit it may have been, but for a pain-filled loser like me, it was the most effective way of ensuring that I made some impact on someone, sometimes.

I'm sure people were infuriated by my sardonic attitude. I don't blame them. But I think if they'd known what a yearning there was within me to give and receive warmth and emotion at exactly the same time as I was attempting to cut every other ego in sight down to size, they would have been amazed.

With a few friends, predictably those who demonstrated unequivocally that they valued me, I dropped my act, but those people were few and far between.

A significant effect of encounters with God over the last few years has, thank goodness, been a release of the natural, childlike desire in me to love and be loved for what I am, however unimpressive that turns out to be. I believe and hope that my sarcasm has been transfigured into satire nowadays. As I read today's passage I see and sense in the heart of it God's promise that all the locked, beautiful gardens within us will be thrown open one day, and all the sealed fountains allowed to overflow with feelings and thoughts and words that have hardly seen the light of day before. I know that some of you who are reading these words today need that more than anything else in the world.

### Prayer

*Unlock us and release us, Lord. Walk in this garden. Drink from this fountain.*
*AP*

Song of Solomon 5:8–11, 16 (NIV)

# *What do you think about God?*

O daughters of Jerusalem, I charge you—if you find my lover, what will you tell him? Tell him I am faint with love. How is your beloved better than others, most beautiful of women? How is your beloved better than others, that you charge us so? My lover is radiant and ruddy, outstanding among ten thousand. His head is purest gold; his hair is wavy and black as a raven... His mouth is sweetness itself; he is altogether lovely. This is my lover, this my friend, O daughters of Jerusalem.

Because of travelling so much as a speaker I see an enormous number of churches in the course of a year, and I meet hundreds of Christians doing work of various kinds, from full-time ministry to the making of coffee on a Sunday morning. I never tire of hearing what's happening, especially from people who are really caught up in their activities. James Herriot wrote that enthusiasts are attractive, but fanatics are irresistible. I agree. Quite often, though, when I have been listening for some time to a description of recent youth-group activities or progress with the new church extension, I throw in a question that I've asked more times than I've had cold dinners that were supposed to be hot at missionary fund-raising meetings.

'What do you think about God?'

The usual reply, after a moment's puzzled silence, is, 'What do you mean?'

'Well, what do you personally think and feel about God—about Jesus?'

Some people wouldn't be able to answer this question if I stood and waited all day, because, at this stage in their lives, they have not met him in any conscious sense. Others speak with varying degrees of eagerness or devotion, but the ones I really enjoy are those whose eyes and manner soften, as they attempt, however incoherently or lucidly, to tell me how much they love him, and, perhaps, how proud they are to be working for him.

That's more or less what is happening in this passage.

'What's so special about this man of yours?' the women ask.

The reply is lyrical and overwhelming, containing words that, for two thousand years, have summed up the feelings of true believers about Jesus.

'This is my beloved and this is my friend.'

### Prayer

*Help us to put you at the centre of our work for you, Lord, and to give a good, warm account of you when we are asked.*

AP

### Song of Solomon 6:1–5 (NIV)

# Open our eyes

Where has your lover gone, most beautiful of women? Which way did your lover turn, that we may look for him with you? My lover has gone down to his garden, to the beds of spices, to browse in the gardens and to gather lilies. I am my lover's and my lover is mine; he browses among the lilies. You are beautiful, my darling, as Tirzah, lovely as Jerusalem, majestic as troops with banners. Turn your eyes from me; they overwhelm me. Your hair is like a flock of goats descending from Gilead.

Have you ever wondered why God has allowed Mother Teresa to become known to such a wide public? Wouldn't it have made more sense to leave her to quietly get on with her work among the poor in India, while the blow-wave evangelists do all the up-front stuff. Clearly, God wanted to make some sort of point, and this passage may offer a clue as to what it was.

'Where has your beloved gone?'

When that question is asked of Christians you can expect a wide variety of responses. Some are quite sure he is contained within a specific liturgical framework, others just know that the only venue at which he can be reliably expected to put in an appearance is their very own church between ten-thirty and twelve o'clock on a Sunday morning. Yet others have him stuck down solidly to the pages of the Bible, a number are certain he lives at Butlins, and there are even a few who would locate him somewhere inside a television set, firmly under the control of a steely-eyed American evangelist.

What would Mother Teresa say? I suspect that she might reply in a rather similar way to the maiden in these verses, that he has gone to pasture his flocks in the gardens. But for Mother Teresa the flocks are sick, filth-ingrained, homeless people, and the gardens are the teeming streets of India. I believe that God raised this remarkable woman to prominence to remind us that our beloved is still to be found among those who need him, and to help us understand that if our spiritual sight is corrected we might be able, like Mother Teresa, to see Jesus in the eyes of beggars, and lilies on the streets of Calcutta.

### Prayer

*Open the eyes of our understanding, Lord, to see where you are to be found. May we see hope where there was only despair, and beauty where there was only ugliness.*

AP

## Song of Solomon 7:1–2, 6–9 (NIV)

# *On the contrary*

How beautiful your sandalled feet, O prince's daughter! Your graceful legs are like jewels, the work of a craftsman's hands. Your navel is a rounded goblet that never lacks blended wine. Your waist is a mound of wheat encircled by lilies... How beautiful you are and how pleasing, O love, with your delights! Your stature is like that of the palm, and your breasts like clusters of fruit. I said, 'I will climb the palm tree; I will take hold of its fruit.' May your breasts be like the clusters of the vine, the fragrance of your breath like apples, and your mouth like the best wine. May the wine go straight to my lover, flowing gently over lips and teeth.

Solomon must have been a wow at Old Testament parties, mustn't he? What a chat-up line! I wonder how he would have got on nowadays. I'm not sure how the average modern girl would react to being told that her navel is a rounded bowl that never lacks mixed wine. I'm a bit confused about the rounded thighs like jewels as well. Jewels? I expect those references had cultural significance. The rest of this passage, though—my goodness!

If those who condemn the Bible (without reading it) for being bland and passionless were to study passages like this, they might have to shift their attack to a different front altogether. Perhaps they would end up complaining that such blatantly sensual expressions of sexual desire are inappropriate to a book claiming to be the living word of God. After all, they might point out, he is uncompromisingly critical of sexual immorality in many other parts of the very same book. But, of course, that is precisely the point. Sadly, the Church

has tended to emphasize the negative aspects of sex, so that for many it has become an area of dark repression and guilt. God is often perceived as being concerned only with preventing people from enjoying themselves.

Read the passage again. Allegorically or literally, its message is clear. This climber of palm trees, this holder of branches, this connoisseur of wines and kisses, is as far removed from being anti-sex as it is possible to be. God is not just mildly and benignly tolerant of physical love, he is extravagantly in favour of it when it is enjoyed within the context of a spiritually committed relationship. He designed it, and saw that it was good. And it is.

### Prayer

*Lord, help us not to be frightened about things that you have given us. We'll try to be positive when talking about these things to people who don't know you.*

AP

Song of Solomon 7:10–13 (NIV)

# *Nowhere in particular*

I belong to my lover, and his desire is for me. Come, my lover, let us go to the countryside, let us spend the night in the villages. Let us go early to the vineyards to see if the vines have budded, if their blossoms have opened, and if the pomegranates are in bloom—there I will give you my love. The mandrakes send out their fragrance, and at our door is every delicacy, both new and old, that I have stored up for you, my lover.

A few weeks before writing this note, Bridget and I took David and Katy over to France to spend a few days at the small cottage in Normandy that we own jointly with some local friends. This dumpy little dwelling, blessedly lacking in everything beginning with the prefix 'tele', stands next to a tiny junior school in a sleepy village, and has only three rooms, one dining-sitting-doing-things sort of room, and two bedrooms. The optimistically named 'bathroom' is designed for people at the lower end of the not-very-tall range, but it allows you to do whatever you need to do, albeit in rather contorted postures.

Ours is not a smart cottage. It probably qualifies for a quarter-star rating, but it and the fascinatingly lit valley it overlooks are full of strong magic. Those who stay there invariably seem to relax, and that's exactly what we did on this occasion.

I'm potty about France anyway, but there was something extra special about this visit. Something inside me sat down and took it easy for the first time for a very long time. We went for little walks to nowhere in particular, we cycled through farms to a place where the river runs beneath an old crumbling bridge and talked to a little brown goat who seemed anxious to get to know us, we went up to the nearby forest and collected kindling for the open fire, we ate long lingering breakfasts at the table by the window that overlooks the valley and we played french cricket on the lawn (an area of rough grass at the side of the house).

Something about this passage is almost tearfully reminiscent of those all too few peaceful days when we laughed together and looked at things together and simply rejoiced in being people who loved each other in a place that was lovely. It doesn't happen very often, does it? When the Lord and his bride are truly united it will happen for ever and ever.

A prayer

*Come soon, Lord Jesus.*

AP

Song of Solomon 8:6–7 (NIV)

# *Permission to feel*

Place me like a seal over your heart, like a seal on your arm; for love is as strong as death, its jealousy unyielding as the grave. It burns like blazing fire, like a mighty flame. Many waters cannot quench love; rivers cannot wash it away. If one were to give all the wealth of his house for love, it would be utterly scorned.

What do you think about unreliable people? I'm infuriatingly erratic at times. Kind people who write to me might get a reply the very next day, or they might end up sending me one of those embarrassing little following notes that say: 'I enclose a copy of the letter I sent to you last year, as the original was clearly lost in the post...'

Unreliable people are maddening at times (I have a degree in Hypocrisy), but they can also be vivid and stimulating. When options are not obliged to arrange themselves in straight lines, anything can happen, with wonderful or terrible results.

The same is true of emotions. When I was a young Christian we were 'warned off' emotions, as though they were dangerous ogres, sitting on our shoulders, whispering deceitful distractions to lure us from the straight and narrow. Generally speaking, I accepted this caution, but I was a bit puzzled. Why, when my original encounter with Jesus had been such an emotional affair, and I was such an emotional person who felt everything so deeply, was I supposed to ignore feelings?

Nowadays, I see the defensiveness that probably crept into such teaching. At those times when God cannot be seen, heard, touched, smelled, tasted or otherwise sensed in any way, the only thing likely to rein in your average youth group is a previously implanted suggestion that the way you feel, however dismal, has no real relevance to the situation. And, yes, there is a real, crucially important point to be made about trusting what you know, at the times when you stop feeling it. But one of the things that the Song of Songs in general, and this passage in particular, teaches us, is that because God's love affair with the church is a passionate, emotional business, feelings are an essential part of our relationship with him.

Like those unreliable friends, our emotions have an alarming, but necessary and potentially very creative role in our spiritual lives. Be wary by all means, but not wooden.

A prayer

*Open our eyes and our hearts, Lord, to your love, strong as death, your passion, fierce as the grave.*

AP

INTRODUCTION
# Genesis

Genesis is Greek for 'beginning' and the name of this book is taken from the first significant word in the old Greek translation of the Old Testament. Quite simply, that is what the book is about.

It tells of the beginning of the world, and the beginning of the Hebrew people and nation. It probably reached its final form after the return from exile in Babylon, say about the fourth century BC. Much of it, though is far older. It comprises folk tales of the origin of God's people, myths and legends of creation and prehistory, woven into a narrative that tells of God's purposes for the world and for his people.

To speak of parts of the book as myth and legend is worrying for some Christians. They feel that if the book is not 'true' then it cannot be the word and God, and that this also calls into question the truth of other parts of the Bible, such as the Gospels themselves.

However, such fears are groundless. The Bible is a library, not a single book, and in that library are books of poetry, law, proverbs, prophecy, history, romance, folklore—yes, and myths and legends. Each needs to be recognized for what it is, and read in an appropriate way. When we take this approach, we soon realize that there is indeed one common centre to the whole of Scripture; it bears witness to God, his relationship with his people, and his promise of salvation.

So there is no need, for instance, to try to take the creation accounts of Genesis 1 and 2 literally. Quite possibly the final compiler of the book realized that too, for the two accounts are incompatible. Yet both convey a real truth—that the world is the work of God, and as such is neither pointless nor without value. And that God has been concerned with all he made from long before the dawn of human history—and will still be involved with his creation long after history ends.

*Marcus Maxwell*

Genesis 1:1–5 (NRSV)

# Beginnings

In the beginning, when God created the heavens and the earth, the earth was a formless void and darkness covered the face of the deep, while a wind from God swept over the face of the waters. Then God said, 'Let there be light'; and there was light. And God saw that the light was good; and God separated the light from the darkness. God called the light Day, and the darkness he called Night. And there was evening and there was morning, the first day.

The Hebrew word here translated 'created' is only ever used of the activity of God. When God creates, he does something that no human being can do. He makes things which depend for their continuing existence on him alone. Right at the beginning of the Bible, we are told that all things depend on God, and are there because he, in some sense, wills them to be.

It's a far cry from the prevailing attitude to the world today. We are told that the world exists by chance (and a pretty remote chance at that), that as a result it is basically purposeless, and therefore pointless. I can't help feeling that it is this philosophy, though rarely expressed by most people, which lies at the root of the sense of despair that so many feel.

Genesis tells us otherwise. The universe is created, in all its incalculable vastness, by God, and as such has a purpose and a destiny. This is not to deny that many of the mechanisms of creation may well work by random events and natural selection. It is rather to say that God's creation has an inbuilt mechanism which allows it to change and adapt, to produce its own wonders, all within the creative purposes of God.

We are not told here what those purposes are, though elsewhere we discover that they are about giving glory to God. Here it is enough to know that what God made was good, and to give thanks to him for it.

## Meditate

*Then I heard every creature in heaven and on earth and under the earth and in the sea, and all that is in them, singing, 'To the one seated on the throne, and to the Lamb, be blessing and honour and glory and might, forever and ever!' (Revelation 5:13)*

MM

Genesis 1:11–25 (parts) (NRSV)

# Design

Then God said, 'Let the earth put forth vegetation: plants yielding seed, and fruit trees of every kind on earth that bear fruit with the seed in it.' And it was so.... And God saw that it was good.... And God said, 'Let the waters bring forth swarms of living creatures, and let birds fly across the dome of the sky.' So God created the great sea monsters and every living creature that moves, of every kind, with which the waters swarm, and every winged bird of every kind. And God saw that it was good.... And God said, 'Let the earth bring forth living creatures of every kind: cattle and creeping things and wild animals of the earth of every kind.' And it was so.... And God saw that it was good.

I've occasionally heard preachers suggest that, while we can't take Genesis 1 as a literal account of creation, none the less it gives a progressive account of the way in which life developed on earth. In fact, it doesn't, even if we leave out the accounts of the creation of the sun, moon and stars as we have done.

What it does give possibly the earliest ever attempt to classify living things into discrete groups. (And for that matter, it uses a method similar to one very modern system of classification, though in a very rough and ready way.) And this tells us something very important about God. He is orderly and rational.

God does not create capriciously, nor does he bend the rules. He creates an ordered system which follows understandable laws and which rational minds (created by the rational God) can understand, however incompletely. The beginning of the Bible assures us that God is not someone who plays games. It is the first statement of one of the great biblical themes: God can be relied upon.

It has often been pointed out that this is one reason why modern science developed in the West. It was there that Jews, Christians and Muslims shared the conviction that a rational god had created an orderly world. And an orderly world is still the basic tenet of faith held by modern scientists.

## Reflect

*For us, this conviction is more personally important; we can trust God. Written across the face of creation itself is the message that God is trustworthy. We may not always understand him, or what he does, but if we give ourselves to his care, he can be relied on.*

MM

### Genesis 1:26–27, 29–31 (NRSV)

# Image and dominion

Then God said, 'Let us make humankind in our image, according to our likeness; and let them have dominion over the fish of the sea, and over the birds of the air, and over the cattle, and over all the wild animals of the earth, and over every creeping thing that creeps upon the earth.' So God created humankind in his image, in the image of God he created them, male and female he created them. God blessed them... God said, 'See, I have given you every plant yielding seed that is upon the face of all the earth, and every tree with seed in its fruit; you shall have them for food. And to every beast of the earth, and to every bird of the air, and to everything that creeps on the earth, everything that has the breath of life, I have given every green plant for food.' And it was so. God saw everything that he had made, and indeed, it was very good.

The first story of creation draws to a climax, with the creation of God's crowning achievement – human beings. Many would not see it that way. Of all the animal kingdom, humans alone wage war, kill for sheer pleasure, exterminate other species on a daily basis, and destroy the very environment on which they depend for their existence. On the other hand, humans alone create art, wonder at the fact of their very being, and worship.

And both the good and the bad of being human is to do with two words whose meaning is far from clear: image and dominion. What does it mean to be made in the image of God? There is something people have in common with God which no other earthly creature has. And frustratingly, we are not told exactly what it is. Perhaps that is deliberate. Some have argued that it is free will, or responsibility, or creativity.

I suspect that it is no single quality. However we exactly define it, the image of God is what makes us able to relate consciously to God. And consciously to disobey him.

When we do that, we spoil both the image of God and our dominion of the earth, turning it from the careful rule of stewards into the tyranny of conquerors. Despite the way it has sometimes been taken, dominion over creation is not a mandate to abuse, but to care for creation.

### Meditate

*You have stripped off the old self... and have clothed yourselves with the new self, which is being renewed in knowledge according to the image of its creator.*

Colossians 3:10

MM

## Genesis 2:4b–9 (NRSV)

# *Life*

In the day that the Lord God made the earth and the heavens, when no plant of the field was yet in the earth and no herb of the field had yet sprung up—for the Lord God had not caused it to rain upon the earth, and there was no one to till the ground; but a stream would rise from the earth, and water the whole face of the ground—then the Lord God formed man from the dust of the ground, and breathed into his nostrils the breath of life; and the man became a living being. And the Lord God planted a garden in Eden, in the east; and there he put the man whom he had formed. Out of the ground the Lord God made to grow every tree that is pleasant to the sight and good for food, the tree of life also in the midst of the garden, and the tree of the knowledge of good and evil.

The second, and older, creation story is very different from that of Genesis 1. Yet there are important similarities. There is no mention of the image of God, but instead, we are told that God breathed his breath/spirit into the man to bring him to life. Later, God creates the animals but there is no mention of the breath of life. The animating principle of human beings is more than mere biological life. There is a spiritual dimension without which human beings might perhaps live, but would not be truly, spiritually, alive.

Nowadays there are two very different mistakes which people make about our role in creation. The first, and older one, is to say that since we have the ability to control the world, and the demonstrable superiority of intelligence and so on, we have every right to see ourselves as lords and mistresses of all we survey. The second view sees human beings as simply another species of animal, with no greater rights than the rest, and as being (as we considered yesterday) the greatest threat to the world.

Genesis 2 won't allow us to take either option. The man and the animals are all made from the dust of the earth, and so are of the same stuff. Humanity is part of creation, and dependent on it. Yet there is that spiritual dimension which is uniquely ours, which gives us awareness of God and with it, responsibility to him for the rest of creation.

### Reflect

*Human beings have the possibility of becoming the world's nervous system—or its cancer.*

Jürgen Moltmann

MM

Genesis 2:18–24 (part) (NRSV)

# *Togetherness*

Then the Lord God said, 'It is not good that the man should be alone; I will make him a helper as his partner.' So out of the ground the Lord God formed every animal... and every bird of the air... The man gave names to all cattle, and to the birds of the air, and to every animal... but for the man there was not found a helper as his partner. So the Lord God caused a deep sleep to fall upon the man, and he slept; then he took one of his ribs and closed up its place with flesh. And the rib that the Lord God had taken from the man he made into a woman and brought her to the man. Then the man said, 'This at last is bone of my bones and flesh of my flesh; this one shall be called Woman, for out of Man this one was taken.' Therefore a man leaves his father and his mother and clings to his wife, and they become one flesh. And the man and his wife were both naked and were not ashamed.

'I am a rock,' sang Paul Simon, 'I am an island, and a rock feels no pain, and an island never cries.' It was a song recognizing what Genesis had recognized long before; that it is not good for human beings to live alone. Save for a few who may be called into solitary fellowship with God, being alone is a recipe for human stagnation and a shrivelling of the soul. People are made to live together. The closest relationship is seen as that between a man and a woman, and the passage is rightly seen as laying the foundation for a Christian understanding of marriage (both Jesus and Paul quoted it).

Yet is is a mistake to relate it only to marriage, for its implications are far wider. It tells of the need for mutual help (the term 'helper' does not imply any form of inferiority). It tells of a need for openness with others, for the naked-

ness referred to is not merely physical. Here is a picture of people able to reveal their true selves to one who is there to help and support. And that is the basis of true community. In the story, sin, shame and blame are about to enter. But it sets a pattern to aspire to, especially for the Church which is called to be the community of Christ's people. In the church there must be the extra dimension of forgiveness. There is no return to innocence, but there can, with God's help, be a striving after mutual support, acceptance and forgiveness. Then God's people will have a pattern to offer to the world.

### Pray

*Give us acceptance of one another, that we may learn to be each other's helpers.*
*MM*

### Genesis 3:1–7 (parts) (NRSV)

# *Snake in the grass*

Now the serpent was more crafty than any other wild animal that the Lord God had made. He said to the woman, 'Did God say, "You shall not eat from any tree in the garden?"' The woman said to the serpent, 'We may eat of the fruit of the trees in the garden; but God said, "You shall not eat of the fruit of the tree that is in the middle of the garden, nor shall you touch it, or you shall die."' But the serpent said to the woman, 'You will not die; for God knows that when you eat of it, your eyes will be opened, and you will be like God, knowing good and evil.' So... she took of its fruit and ate; and she also gave some to her husband, who was with her, and he ate. Then the eyes of both were opened, and they knew that they were naked; and they sewed fig leaves together and made loincloths for themselves.

This is a fable, with a much more serious point than any of Aesop's. It is a fable which tells of the roots of sin. The tree has been forbidden (perhaps only temporarily, since its presence in the garden suggests eventual use) but it looks attractive, and above all, it offers the gift of wisdom.

So the man and the woman eat. Interestingly, the passage has been taken to suggest that women are more prone to sin than men (see 1 Timothy 2:14). In fact, in the story, the woman is the only one to put up an objection (though the man is there), and becomes the first person in the Bible to expound the word of God.

So they eat, and gain knowledge. 'Knowledge of good and evil' is a Hebrew way of saying, the whole span of knowledge from good to evil. For that is the real temptation; to 'become like God' by the pursuit of knowledge alone. Sin in essence is the attempt to become self-made and forget the need to rely on God. But their eyes become opened to more than abstract knowledge. They gain another kind. They already knew right and wrong, as the serpent's conversation shows. But now they experience the bitter reality of guilt, and can no longer bear to be exposed to each other. They hide figuratively behind clothes, as they will hide literally from God. There is some knowledge, gained by experience, which it is far better never to have, for it builds barriers between people, and between us and God.

Pray

*Father, for all the experience I would rather have missed, forgive me and restore me.*

MM

### Mark 2:13–17 (NEB)

# Who needs a doctor?

[Jesus] went away to the lake-side. All the crowd came to him, and he taught them there. As he went along, he saw Levi son of Alphaeus at his seat in the custom-house, and said to him, 'Follow me'; and Levi rose and followed him. When Jesus was at table in his house, many bad characters—tax-gatherers and others—were seated with him and his disciples; for there were many who followed him. Some doctors of the law who were Pharisees noticed him eating in this bad company, and said to his disciples, 'He eats with tax gatherers and sinners!' Jesus overheard and said to them, 'It is not the healthy that need a doctor, but the sick; I did not come to invite virtuous people, but sinners.'

Jesus does not, of course, mean that there are some who can do without him. But there are those who know their need, and like the sick person calling for a doctor turn to him to be healed. Then there are those who feel no need. Secure in their religious righteousness, or their good fortune or their financial stability, they see no need for forgiveness, or for the drastic change of life which comes to those who hear and heed Christ's call to follow him.

The nagging suspicion is that many of Jesus's followers are closer to the Pharisees than to the tax collectors. Rectitude and propriety are the mark of the church, rather than delight that God should spend time and effort on sinners such as us.

So we look askance at those who come into church differently attired, or who make the wrong responses or who simply make a noise out of turn. We look with disapproval at the notorious sinners, and the message of acceptance and forgiveness becomes something to be read about in the Bible, but not something to be lived by Christ's church today.

So from time to time we need to go back to basics; to look at ourselves as sinners rather than the righteous, and discover again the amazing grace of our God. Tax collector or Pharisee? Given a choice, which would you rather be?

MM

**Genesis 3:8–13 (NRSV)**

# *Hiding*

They heard the sound of the Lord God walking in the garden... and the man and his wife hid themselves from the presence of the Lord God among the trees... But the Lord God called to the man and said to him, 'Where are you?' He said, 'I heard the sound of you in the garden, and I was afraid, because I was naked; and I hid myself.' He said, 'Who told you that you were naked? Have you eaten from the tree of which I commanded you not to eat?' The man said, 'The woman whom you gave to be with me, she gave me fruit from the tree, and I ate.' Then the Lord God said to the woman, 'What is this that you have done?' The woman said, 'The serpent tricked me, and I ate.'

This little episode is pregnant with meaning. On the face of it, it is full of acute observation. Like children, the couple hide, hoping their disobedience will go unnoticed, but the very act of hiding is a dead give-away. They now know shame. And God is not fooled. On another level, it is the tale of how human beings hide from God. Failing to acknowledge their sinfulness, they end by failing to acknowledge the one who both convicts of sin, and has the power to heal it. Flight from God is flight from responsibility, a refusal to own the consequences of our own deeds. And it is always a flight from life.

Even when faced with the fact of their disobedience, the human couple pass the buck. The man is the more ingenious. The woman you gave—in the end it is God who is to blame. He should never have put the fly in the ointment. And don't we love to turn arguments around that way? When someone catches us out, isn't the first line of defence to point the finger right back again? Anything rather than take responsibility. But it won't work. The serpent may have tempted, the woman may have given the fruit, but the man and his wife each made a choice, and now they must live with it.

Traditionally, the serpent is seen as the devil. Probably that was not the original intention of the story-teller, but it is a fair interpretation. The devil tempts and corrupts, but it is humans who sin. 'The serpent tricked me,' is no excuse. The story is the tale of how God makes people face up to their own deeds and, as we shall see, he takes stern action. But we shall also see that it is a healing action.

Prayer

*God, give me grace to own my own deeds and misdeeds, to be corrected by you, and brought to salvation.*

*MM*

Genesis 3:14–19 (NRSV)

# *Labour*

The Lord God said to the serpent, 'Because you have done this, cursed are you among all animals...' To the woman he said, 'I will greatly increase your pangs in childbearing; in pain you shall bring forth children, yet your desire shall be for your husband, and he shall rule over you.' And to the man he said, 'Because you have listened to the voice of your wife, and have eaten of the tree about which I commanded you, 'You shall not eat of it,' cursed is the ground because of you; in toil you shall eat of it all the days of your life; thorns and thistles it shall bring forth for you; and you shall eat the plants of the field. By the sweat of your face you shall eat bread until you return to the ground, for out of it you were taken; you are dust, and to dust you shall return.

All human actions have consequences, and sin is no different. Its effects ripple outwards, affecting people and things we could never foresee. So for the writer of Genesis, all creation is out of kilter as a result of human rebellion against God. Here the story is at its most profound. In our age we are more and more coming to see the world as a huge single system, in which ecology, geological movement and human activity play their part for better or for worse. Genesis reminds us that God too is a part of the system and if he is ignored, the system malfunctions.

A reason is given too, for the sense of alienation or dislocation people have when they view the world. Surely things could be better? Yes, they could, but sin has set them awry. We have to live with the consequences of that, but it does not mean that we have to accept them. To deal with the problems the world throws up is right and proper. The danger is to continue in the original sin of believing we can do it alone, disregarding God's will for the world.

The story also invites us to challenge our assumptions about our society. Written from a male dominated culture, the story tells us that the dominance of men over women is the result, not of divine intention, but of sin. How many of the things we take for granted are also the consequences of wrongdoing, and need to be challenged? We are called again to examine all that we do, as individuals and societies, and subject them to a biblical judgment.

### A thought

*Some churchmen objected to the use of anaesthetics in childbirth as being against God's will. They didn't object to agricultural machines. I wonder why?*

MM

## Genesis 3:20–24 (NRSV)

# *Promise and punishment*

The man named his wife Eve, because she was the mother of all living. And the Lord God made garments of skins for the man and for his wife, and clothed them. Then the Lord God said, 'See, the man has become like one of us, knowing good and evil; and now, he might reach out his hand and take also from the tree of life, and eat, and live for ever'—therefore the Lord God sent him forth from the garden of Eden, to till the ground from which he was taken. He drove out the man; and at the east of the garden of Eden he placed the cherubim, and a sword flaming and turning to guard the way to the tree of life.

The result of disobedience is death. Not instant annihilation, but the loss of the promise of eternal life symbolized by the tree of life. This is both punishment and help. For if the man and woman were able to live eternally in a state of rebellion against God, they would no longer be human. Nor would they be divine. They may be like gods in their knowledge, but not in their morals. The sentence of death is salvation from the possibility of demonic existence.

But God has not given up on his beloved creatures. Now that they are knowingly naked, they need clothes, so God provides better garments than those they had made themselves. And in this he demonstrates the care that people will know from God through the rest of the Bible. For now, the way to eternal life is closed, barred by a flaming sword, and guarded by angels. But it will not always be so. There is a long and painful journey ahead, but there is hope for rebellious humanity.

There are deeper depths to which they will sink, and unimaginable evils will be perpetrated. But in the midst of this, God will call a man, and then a people, to live for him in the world. And in the end, he will walk among them again, not to enjoy the evening breeze, but to feel the impact of nails.

The tree of life is lost for a time, but it reappears at the end – the promise of eternal life is opened through the grimmer tree of Calvary.

### Reflect

*Then the angel showed me the river of the water of life, bright as crystal, flowing from the throne of God and of the Lamb through the middle of the street of the city. On either side of the river is the tree of life with its twelve kinds of fruit, producing its fruit each month; and the leaves of the tree are for the healing of the nations.*

Revelation 22:1–2

*MM*

### Genesis 4:1–7 (NRSV)

# *Temptation again*

Now the man knew his wife Eve, and she conceived and bore Cain, saying, 'I have produced a man with the help of the Lord.' Next she bore his brother Abel. Now Abel was a keeper of sheep, and Cain a tiller of the ground. In the course of time Cain brought to the Lord an offering of the fruit of the ground, and Abel for his part brought of the firstlings of his flock, their fat portions. And the Lord had regard for Abel and his offering, but for Cain and his offering he had no regard. So Cain was very angry and his countenance fell. The Lord said to Cain, 'Why are you angry, and why has your countenance fallen? If you do well, will you not be accepted? And if you do not do well, sin is lurking at the door; its desire is for you, but you must master it.'

Out in the wide world, the human race begins to grow and prosper, and for all the disastrous beginnings, God is not forgotten. He remains humanity's creator and protector, and the object of their love and worship. But that love and worship is not always whole-hearted. We are not told explicitly why Cain's sacrifice was unacceptable to God, but there is strong hint in the descriptions of the offerings. Abel gives the fat (that is, best,) portions of the first of his flock, while Cain gives simply an offering. Perhaps the difference is like the one we can find in any church on a Sunday morning; there are those who give a considered and sacrificial offering in the collection, and those who dig in for the first bit of loose change. Cain will sacrifice, but it is a token nod to God. And God is not fooled.

However that might be, the writer again shows that he understands human nature. Cain's response is anger rather than repentance. He knows full well that he is in the wrong, but once again, it is easier to hide than to accept responsibility. This time, he hides in hatred.

God's challenge is to own up to the real problem, to accept failure and grow through it to the mastery of the sin that dominates the one who takes refuge in anger. It is a strange irony that one of the most common criticisms of Christianity is that it encourages people to hide from reality. In actual fact it is a constant challenge to face the hardest reality—one's own self, so that we may turn to God and be brought to maturity.

### Pray

*Father, help me to face myself, but to do it in your strength, and by your grace be transformed into true maturity.*

MM

**Genesis 4. 8–16 (NRSV)**

# Death and grace

Cain said to his brother Abel, 'Let us go out to the field.' And when they were in the field, Cain rose up against his brother Abel and killed him. Then the Lord said to Cain, 'Where is your brother Abel?' He said, 'I do not know; am I my brother's keeper?' And the Lord said, 'What have you done? Listen; your brother's blood is crying out to me from the ground! And now you... will be a fugitive and wanderer on the earth.' Cain said to the Lord, 'My punishment is greater than I can bear! Today you have driven me away from the soil, and I shall be hidden from your face; I shall be a fugitive and a wanderer on the earth, and anyone who meets me may kill me.' Then the Lord said to him, 'Not so! Whoever kills Cain will suffer a seven-fold vengeance.' And the Lord put a mark on Cain so that no one who came upon him would kill him. Then Cain went away from the presence of the Lord, and settled in the land of Nod, east of Eden.

The human story continues with the first murder. On the face of it, it is the tale of how anger and guilt solidify into envy and hatred. It's a process all of us are familiar with, though rarely so violently. We are also given a contrast between Cain's actual deed, and his real responsibility. His response to God rings with bitter irony; am I my brother's keeper? God's answer is yes, indeed you are! It is a question people still ask, and still expect the answer Cain wanted. But God's answer remains the same. It is more difficult to be our brother's keeper than his killer. It is easier to be envious of the more successful, fearful of the stranger, resentful of the foreigner. But we are still confronted with God's demand.

Yet for all his dreadful sin, Cain stands under God's protection. Cain no doubt deserves to die for his sin, but for others to slay him is only to increase the cycle of violence. Dead, Cain can do nothing. Alive, he can be brought to repentance and can contribute something to make up for his act. Is this justice? we may well ask. No it is not. It is grace. And before we cry too loudly for justice, let us ask whether the time may not come when we too will need grace. It is no surprise then, to discover that the mark on Cain is traditionally shown as a cross.

Pray

*Lord, give me grace, not justice, and help me to share that grace with my brother, whoever he may be.*

MM

77

### Genesis 4:17–26 (NRSV)

# *Blood and iron*

Cain knew his wife, and she conceived and bore Enoch; and he built a city... To Enoch was born Irad; and Irad was the father of Mehujael, and Mehujael the father of Methushael, and Methushael the father of Lamech. Lamech took two wives; the name of one was Adah, the name of the other Zillah. Adah bore Jabal; he was the ancestor of those who live in tents and have livestock. His brother's name was Jubal; he was the ancestor of all those who play the lyre and pipe. Zillah bore Tubal-cain, who made all kinds of bronze and iron tools... Lamech said... 'Adah and Zillah, hear my voice; you wives of Lamech listen to what I say; I have killed a man for wounding me, a young man for striking me. If Cain is avenged sevenfold, truly Lamech seventy-sevenfold.'

We need not ask where Cain's wife came from, much less the population of his city. This is the realm of myth, and the meaning is not found on the literal level. Instead, we are pointed to the results of God's mercy. Because Cain lived, the foundations of civilization were laid. From his line come the skills of herdsmen, city-dwellers, musicians and metal-workers.

Is this a condemnation of technology and civilization, suggesting that these so-called developments are founded on blood? Or is it a celebration of the beneficial effects of God's mercy? In fact, it is both. Cain and his descendants show themselves capable of great things; they develop the origins of science and technology. But with their pride in their achievements comes another pride, which forgets the grace of God. The end of their development is Lamech's bloody boast. The judgment which God reserved for himself in Cain's case is usurped by Lamech, whose wealth and power lead him to repeat the sin of the garden of Eden. What was God's prerogative was claimed by Adam's descendant. And still is.

The writer tells us to look closely at what we make. Is our technology used to the glory of God, or for human sinfulness? Both possibilities are open to us, and in practice both jostle together. Tubal-cain made the first metal tools. Then comes Lamech's claim of the right to kill. What use were those tools put to? What use today do we make of the vast means we have to heal and to destroy, to build and to cast down?

### Pray

*Lord, open our eyes to our achievements, and show us where we need to give you thanks, and where to repent.*

MM

Matthew 4:1–4 (RSV)

# Body and soul

Jesus was led up by the Spirit into the wilderness to be tempted. And he fasted forty days and forty nights, and afterward he was hungry. And the tempter came and said to him, 'If you are the Son of God, command these stones to become loaves of bread.' But he answered, 'It is written, "Man shall not live by bread alone, but by every word that proceeds from the mouth of God."'

The temptation is to reduce everything to the material level. Jesus is hungry, so the need is for bread. Yet there is another hunger he must satisfy; to know and do the will of God.

The next two temptations are the same in essence: to prove his body's invulnerability by a death-defying leap and to conquer the world by force of arms. But to gain any of these material successes, Jesus must deny his calling, his soul, his God.

The temptation Jesus faced is the great temptation of our age, and it comes ever so seductively and reasonably phrased. Why spend money on churches or works of art to decorate them when people starve? Why talk of heaven and eternal life when the need is to cope with the problems of the here and now? Yet if we deny the need for worship, for art, for eternal hope, what is left in the here and now that is worth striving for? We are more than the purely physical, and we deny that extra dimension at our peril.

Yet it is not a stark choice between body and soul. In the Bible there is no such division. People are bodies and they are souls, and each aspect is necessary for a full understanding of humanity. So we affirm both, calling for food for the hungry and nourishment of the spirit. And in our eucharist the two meet, as the food of the flesh becomes the vehicle for the food of the spirit. In communion we draw close to the God who 'is spirit' (John 4:24), and yet is made flesh for us.

*MM*

### Mark 4:35–41 (NIV)

# *Lord of creation*

When evening came, [Jesus] said to his disciples, 'Let us go over to the other side.' Leaving the crowd behind, they took him along... in the boat... A furious squall came up, and the waves broke over the boat, so that it was nearly swamped. Jesus was in the stern, sleeping on a cushion. The disciples woke him and said to him, 'Teacher, don't you care if we drown?' He got up, rebuked the wind and said to the waves, 'Quiet! Be still!' Then the wind died down and it was completely calm. He said to his disciples, 'Why are you so afraid? Do you still have no faith?' They were terrified and asked each other, 'Who is this? Even the wind and the waves obey him!'

Jesus was tired after a day spent teaching a huge crowd. Now, human as he was, he was glad to escape with the small group. But the Sea of Galilee is notorious for its sudden storms. Even the fishermen were scared; they woke him with an angry rebuke—and a sticky situation became a new opportunity for him to demonstrate his power. They had already seen his power to heal, his right to forgive sins and his command over demons. Now they saw his authority over the storm.

That does not surprise us, for Jesus had a major share in the creation of the universe. 'The Son... through whom he made the universe' (Hebrews 1:1); 'By him all things were created; things in heaven and on earth' (Colossians 1:16); 'Without him was not anything made that has been made' (John 1:3). Jesus is Lord over all creation; it was a small thing for him to subdue the squall.

That raises a question. If he has control over the created world, why does he allow the natural disasters that cause so much suffering? The bare bones of the answer is this. God created a good world, and he gave people responsibility to care for it. So when people disobeyed God, not only human nature but creation itself was spoilt. The story of the Fall points to the spoilt creation (Genesis 3:18) and also to the Messiah (3:15). For God does not ignore the suffering; his love sent his Son into the heart of pain. When Jesus' rescue operation in the world is ultimately fulfilled, creation too will be redeemed, 'liberated from the bondage to decay and brought into the glorious freedom of the children of God' (Romans 8:21).

*RG*

Mark 5:1–10 (NIV)

# Gripped by evil

They went... to the region of the Gerasenes... A man with an evil spirit came... to meet him. This man lived in the tombs... He had often been chained hand and foot, but he tore the chains apart and broke the irons on his feet. No-one was strong enough to subdue him. Night and day... he would cry out and cut himself with stones. When he saw Jesus... he ran and fell on his knees in front of him. He shouted... 'What do you want with me, Jesus, Son of the Most High God? Swear to God that you won't torture me!' For Jesus had said to him, 'Come out of this man, you evil spirit!' Then Jesus asked him, 'What is your name?' 'My name is Legion,' he replied, 'for we are many.' And he begged Jesus again and again not to send them out of the area.

Are some readers in 1997 sceptical about this account? 'This man was merely psychiatrically ill; schizophrenia, I expect.' But evil spirits are as real in twentieth-century Western culture as they were in Jesus' time, although they are often more subtle in their activity than in this story. I remember a comment from an occupational therapy student in Oxford after meeting a woman who was deep into witchcraft: 'She gave me the same sensation of prickles on the back of my neck that I get from some* of our psychiatric patients in the hospital; now I know its origin.' She saw that those patients were affected by evil spirits as well as psychiatrically disturbed. Here are some of the features about this man that I have met face to face in the past twenty years.

1) The evil spirits had a deep grip on him. This measure of 'possession' is rare; more often (as with many of the people Jesus met) just one aspect of a person's life has been affected by an evil spirit.

2) He showed supernatural physical strength.

3) The demons had a very destructive influence on his personality and lifestyle.

4) They knew who Jesus was, even when the people around did not.

5) They tried to bargain with him but they could not stand against his authority. Spirits in people today bow to the name of Jesus.

Jesus said, 'The thief comes only to steal and kill and destroy; I have come that they may have life, and have it to the full' (John 10:10).

*RG*

* *Editor's note: NB Only some. Rosemary Green is not saying that all psychiatric illness has demonic origins. M. Scott Peck's* The People of the Lie *is a fascinating set of case histories of patients of his for whose condition he could find no other explanation than the evil power whom the Bible calls 'the father of lies'.*

Mark 5:11–20 (NIV)

# Freed and renewed

[When, under Jesus' control, the spirits left the man they entered a herd of pigs, which then] rushed down the steep bank into the lake and were drowned. Those tending the pigs ran off and reported this... and the people went out to see what had happened. When they came to Jesus, they saw the man who had been possessed by the legion of demons, sitting there, dressed and in his right mind; and they were afraid. Those who had seen it told the people what had happpened to the demon-possessed man—and told about the pigs as well. Then the people began to plead with Jesus to leave their region. As Jesus was getting into the boat, the man who had been demon-possessed begged to go with him. Jesus did not let him, but said, 'Go home to your family and tell them how much the Lord has done for you, and how he has had mercy on you.' So the man went away and began to tell... how much Jesus had done for him. And all the people were amazed.

As this strange, dynamic story continues we notice some other significant features:

1) The man was healed and totally changed. Jesus' power works today to transform people who appear to be 'hopeless cases.'

2) The people were scared, and shrank from things they did not understand. Do we tend to dismiss as 'irrational' events that are outside our own experience and comprehension?

3) The man wanted to stay only with Jesus and his followers. But he had a testimony to share with his family, his friends and with strangers. His changed personality and his life demonstrated what Jesus had done for him, and his words could tell people how it had happened. Our lives and our lips can complement each other to bear witness to what Jesus means to us.

---

### Some questions to ask myself

*Do I expect to see Jesus at work with power? Am I willing to recognize when he works in ways that go beyond my intellectual understanding? What do I have to show other people about the changes he has made in my life? Am I ready to talk about what God means to me?*

RG

## Mark 5:21–24 (NIV)

# *Please come!*

When Jesus had again crossed over by boat to the other side of the lake, a large crowd gathered round him while he was by the lake. Then one of the synagogue rulers, named Jairus, came there. Seeing Jesus, he fell at his feet and pleaded earnestly with him, 'My little daughter is dying. Please come and put your hands on her so that she will be healed and live.' So Jesus went with him. A large crowd followed and pressed around him.

Jesus had made a strong impression in the synagogue, by his teaching, his healing and his exorcism (Mark 1:21–26; 3:1–5) and news of his other miracles had spread fast. Many of the Pharisees were threatened and angry. But Jairus responded differently; his approach to Jesus shows us an example of intercessory prayer.

• 'He fell at his feet.' This man, important in the synagogue, came humbly to Jesus.

• 'He pleaded earnestly.' His concern for his daughter gave intensity to his request. Elijah, too, 'prayed earnestly' (James 5:17); his desire was for God's name to be honoured in Israel. Deep care and concern brings earnestness to our prayers.

• 'My little daughter us dying.' Jairus explained the situation simply. God does not need us to explain every detail to him. He knows already! But when we mention a need to him we express our dependence on him to bring change in the situation.

• 'Please come and put your hands on her.' Jairus longed for Jesus to intervene; he expressed his request plainly but without demanding. It is permissible for us to tell God what we would like him to do, but we have no right to give him orders about how he ought to act.

• 'So that she will be healed.' That shows the expectation of his faith. Jairus had both seen and heard the evidence of Jesus' power to heal, and he trusted that power for his own child.

### A verse to learn

*To encourage us to pray in faith. 'He is the Rock, his works are perfect, and all his ways are just. A faithful God who does no wrong, upright and just is he.'*

Deuteronomy 32:4

RG

Mark 5:25–34 (NIV)

# *Faith in action*

And a woman was there who had been subject to bleeding for twelve years. She had suffered a great deal under the care of many doctors and had spent all she had, yet instead of getting better she grew worse. When she heard about Jesus, she came up behind him in the crowd and touched his cloak... Immediately her bleeding stopped amd she felt in her body that she was freed from her suffering. At once Jesus realised that power had gone out from him.... [He] kept looking around to see who had done it. Then the woman, knowing what had happened to her, came... and, trembling with fear, told him the whole truth. He said to her 'Daughter, your faith has healed you. Go in peace and be freed from your suffering.'

She was ill; she was poor; she was discouraged; she was frightened; her menstrual bleeding made her ceremonially unclean (Leviticus 15:25–28). But she believed, 'if I just touch his clothes, I will be healed' (v. 28). She trusted his power, but she was not sure of his love. Would he care about her, or would he avoid her 'uncleanness'? But faith overcame fear, and she crept up, hoping to be unnoticed by the crowd and by Jesus. She reminds me of many Christians who say in their hearts: 'I know God loves everyone, but does he really want to bother about ME?'

This incident encourages us when we feel like that. Not only was she healed when her faith moved her to action, but Jesus showed his understanding and personal care for her. He was not content for her to slip away silently but persevered in asking 'Who touched me?' until she came forward. He knew that power had gone out from him to heal her body. He also knew her inner need; her shame, her isolation, her sense of rejection. They would be overcome when she acknowledged her need out loud. It was hard for her; but he made her come out into the open because he knew what she most needed. Then he could affirm publicly 'Your faith has healed you. Go in peace.'

### To think over

*'If you confess with your mouth, "Jesus is Lord," and believe in your heart that God raised him from the dead, you will be saved' (Romans 10:9). Public confession of our faith in Jesus is an essential element of being a Christian.*

RG

### Mark 5:35–43 (NIV)

# *Power and compassion*

While Jesus was still speaking, some men came from the house of Jairus, the synagogue ruler. 'Your daughter is dead,' they said. 'Why bother the teacher any more?' Ignoring what they said, Jesus told [him], 'Don't be afraid; just believe.' He did not let anyone follow him except Peter, James and John... When they came to [Jairus'] home, Jesus saw a commotion, with people crying and wailing loudly. He went in and said to them, 'Why all this commotion...? The child is not dead, but asleep.' But they laughed at him. After he put them all out, he took the child's father and mother and the [three] disciples, and went in where the child was. He took her by the hand and said to her 'Little girl, I say to you, get up!' Immediately the girl stood up and walked around... At this they were completely astonished. He gave strict orders not to let anyone know about this, and told them to give her something to eat.

I guess Jairus was pretty agitated by the delay with the bleeding woman, despite the encouragement of seeing her healed of the ailment that had troubled her for as many years as his daughter had lived. Then came the tragic news of her death, delivered without apparent compassion. I think there was an inner tug-of-war between his distress and his faith. But Jesus was totally sensitive to the situation, a sensitivity that he showed in many ways.

1) 'Don't be afraid; just believe.' He understood the turmoil in Jairus' heart.

2) Only the 'special three' were allowed to go with him. This was not a time for a public display of power.

3) He was firm with the mob and their noisy display of emotion, willing to lay himself open to their mocking without telling them what he would do.

4) His power to bring new life was conveyed to the girl very gently. His touch and his words gave a non-dramatic atmosphere for her revival and recovery.

5) His request for food underlined that she was really well—and gave the parents something practical to do.

### A prayer

*Lord Jesus, thank you for your mighty power and your gentle sensitivity. I pray that I may be aware of both in my own life.*

RG

Luke 19:41-48 (NRSV)

# Why Jesus weeps

As Jesus came near and saw the city he wept over it, saying, 'If you, even you, had only recognized on this day the things that make for peace! But now they are hidden from your eyes. Indeed, the days will come upon you, when your enemies will set up ramparts around you and surround you, and hem you in on every side. They will crush you to the ground, you and your children within you, and they will not leave within you one stone upon another; because you did not recognize the time of your visitation from God.' Then he entered the temple and began to drive out those who were selling things there; and he said, 'It is written, "My house shall be a house of prayer"; but you have made it a den of robbers.' Every day he was teaching at the temple. But the chief priests, the teachers of the law and the leaders among the people were trying to kill him. Yet they could not find any way to do it, because all the people hung on his words.

Jesus wept over Jerusalem because they didn't want him and they didn't realize who he was. They preferred darkness to light—and the crucifixion would be their attempt to put out the light of the world.

The temple was the place where God was to be worshipped. Where the people of God were to praise God and to pray to him. But instead they were using the sacrificial system to line their own pockets. The head men of the day had got it disastrously wrong, with the consequence that cracks of destruction were appearing in the system. One day the whole edifice would crash to the ground.

Sunday could be a good day to reflect on our church and to pray for its leaders. Are they getting things right? Are we? How prayerful is the church that we go to. How prayerful are we? How joyful is the church's worship? How joyful is ours? How seriously does the church take the Bible? How seriously do we take it? Is Jesus weeping over us? Or is he delighting in us? We could reflect on the words of the risen Christ to the lukewarm Laodicean church—and perhaps respond to them on behalf of ourself and our church:

'Listen! I am standing at the door, knocking; if you hear my voice and open the door, I will come in to you and eat with you, and you with me' (Revelation 3:20, NRSV).

SB

## Mark 6:1–6 (NIV)

# *Power blocked*

Jesus left [Capernaum] and went to his home town, accompanied by his disciples. When the Sabbath came, he began to teach in the synagogue, and many who heard him were amazed. 'Where did this man get these things?' they asked. 'What's this wisdom that has been given him, that he even does miracles? Isn't this the carpenter? Isn't this Mary's son and the brother of James, Joseph, Judas and Simon? Aren't his sisters here with us?' And they took offence at him. Jesus said to them, 'Only in his home town, among his relatives and in his own house is a prophet without honour.' He could not do any miracles there, except lay his hands on a few sick people and heal them. And he was amazed at their lack of faith.

I imagine that Jesus was looking forward to being back in his Nazareth and with his family. In the synagogue old acquaintances were amazed to hear the depth of wisdom in his teaching. But they could not accept the growth and change they found. Instead they could only look back to the Jesus they had known and to his well-known, working-class family. They could not accept that he had grown out of the known rut and had moved into new paths and new power. It was not just the 'old boy' from Nazareth they were rejecting. It was the Son of God from whom they were turning away. So their scepticism and their hardness of heart blocked his power to heal. On Thursday we read about the woman whose chronic illness healed, to whom Jesus said 'Your faith has healed you.' In Nazareth the opposite was true. We do not read 'he WOULD not do any miracles there' but 'he COULD not do any miracles there.' Faith is a key that unlocks God's mighty power.

Jesus was bitterly disappointed as he left Nazareth. Sadly, there are some church people whose security is so rooted in the familiar that they hold on to the things they know and fail to grasp new wisdom and new ways. Their faith is more in familiar customs than in the living God; then they wonder that God seems unreal, far away and impotent.

---

### To think over

*It is not the quantity of our faith that matters but the quality of our faith in the living God.*

RG

### Mark 6:7–13, 30 (NIV)

# *Empowered for ministry*

Calling the Twelve to him, [Jesus] sent them out two by two and gave them authority over evil spirits. These were his instructions: 'Take nothing for the journey except a staff—no bread, no bag, no money in your belts. Wear sandals but not an extra tunic. Whenever you enter a house, stay there until you leave that town. And if any place will not welcome you or listen to you, shake the dust off your feet when you leave, as a testimony against them. They went out and preached that people should repent. They drove out many demons and anointed many sick people with oil and healed them.

Jesus' disciples had watched him at work in a variety of situations. They had seen his authority and power. They had observed, too, the mixed reactions of people around; some friendly, some hostile. How do you think they felt when they heard they were to go and do the things they had seen their master do? I guess they were both excited and daunted. They were to go in faith, unencumbered by luggage, not knowing who they would meet or where they would stay. They went obediently; they went with Jesus' authority. And they were used with power. When they returned they told him all they had done. Later a larger group went on a similar mission; their amazed, excited news was 'Lord, even the demons submit to us in your name' (Luke 10:17).

What an encouragement for people taking their first steps in active ministry! The short-term missions were preparation for their lives later. Before Jesus finally left them at his ascension he promised his followers 'You will receive power when the Holy Spirit comes upon you; and you wil be my witnesses in Jeruslaem, and in all Judea and Samaria, and to the ends of the earth' (Acts 1:8.) The book of Acts is the story of those same disciples, empowered for a life of mission in preaching, healing and exorcism. We will not all be called to the same sort of ministry; but every Christian is called to be a witness, and the same Spirit of power is available for each one of us.

A prayer

*Lord, what are you calling me to do*
*for you?*

RG

## Mark 6:31–34, 45–46 (NIV)

# *Power replenished*

Because so many people were coming and going that they did not even have a chance to eat, [Jesus] said to [his disciples] 'Come with me by yourselves to a quiet place and get some rest.' So they went away by themselves in a boat to a solitary place. But many who saw them leaving recognised them and ran on foot ... and got there ahead of them. When Jesus landed and saw a large crowd, he had compassion on them, because they were like sheep without a shepherd. So he began teaching them many things... Jesus made his disciples get into the boat and go on ahead of him to Bethsaida, while he dismissed the crowd. After leaving them, he went up a mountainside to pray.

A lecturer in Christian counselling used to write up for the class to see clearly: 'Input = output = input = output.' Jesus knew this lesson well; both for himself and for his followers; the output of active ministry needs to be matched by the input of spiritual refreshment. The Twelve returned from their mission excited and full of news. But the crowd gave them no space, so Jesus took them away to be on their own with him; both bodies and souls needed refreshment. I am writing this on holiday under the African sun while England shivers in the snow! There is much relaxation for body and mind. But I also need to get alone with God if I am to be fully refreshed to return home.

Jesus needed the same refreshment. He was aware of the power that drained out from him in teaching, in miracles, in constant giving to people in need. He, too, needed time alone with his Father. He dismissed the crowd; he sent his disciples off in the boat; 'he went into the hills to pray.'

It is so easy in a busy life to squeeze the time we spend with the Lord. So, before you get busy again today, can I suggest that you spend five minutes (or more) in quietness? Be still and focus on Jesus. You might like to imagine yourself among the group of twelve with him. Or you might choose to picture him alone on the hillside, in two-way communication with his Father. Then allow God to speak to you.

*RG*

89

Mark 7:24–30 (NIV)

# *Openness in prayer*

Jesus left that place and went to the vicinity of Tyre. He entered a house and did not want anyone to know it; yet he could not keep his presence a secret. In fact, as soon as she heard about him, a woman whose little daughter was possessed by an evil spirit came and fell at his feet. The woman was a Greek, born in Syrian Phoenicia. She begged Jesus to drive the demon out of her daughter. 'First let the children eat all they want,' he told her, 'for it is not right to take the children's bread and toss it to their dogs.' 'Yes, Lord,' she replied, 'but even the dogs under the table eat the children's crumbs.' Then he told her, 'For such a reply, you may go; the demon has left your daughter.' She went home and found her child lying on the bed, and the demon gone.

At first sight this story seems to pose a problem. Did Jesus really not care about this non-Jewish woman? Yes, he cared. And, as with each person he met, he knew what was going on inside her. He saw her faith. But he wanted to strengthen that faith by encouraging her persistence. We do not know when the demon left; but her faith enabled Jesus' power to be released at a distance, without any apparent battle. She believed Jesus; she obeyed him; and she found her daughter well.

This story can encourage us when God appears to ignore our prayer. Why is he not complying with my request? Is he not listening? Yes, he is. 'He is always more ready to hear than we are to pray' (Book of Common Prayer). We can be certain that in his love and wisdom he has good purposes when he delays the answer to our pleas.

Some years ago I noticed the radar screens at London airport. They were shaped like slightly curved, bent-back rectangles, and they were constantly turning round through 360 degrees. They showed me how I should be when I pray; open to God, and ready for whatever way he might choose to answer my prayer. Sometimes it is as if I am standing fixed, shouting so hard 'God, why are you not answering me?' that I fail to discern his whisper coming from an unexpected direction.

*RG*

Mark 7:32–37 (NIV)

# *Power for hearing*

Some people brought to him a man who was deaf and could hardly talk, and they begged him to place his hand on the man. After he took him aside, away from the crowd, Jesus put his fingers into the man's ears. Then he spat and touched the man's tongue. He looked up into heaven and with a deep sigh said to him... 'Be opened!' At this, the man's ears were opened, his tongue was loosened and he began to speak plainly. Jesus commanded them not to tell anyone. But the more he did so, the more they kept talking about it. People were overwhelmed with amazement. 'He has done everything well,' they said. 'He even makes the deaf hear and the dumb speak.'

Let us imagine ourselves in the shoes of the man who was deaf and dumb. 'Life's not easy. I feel cut off from people. My eyes are good, and I notice things that others often don't see. But when I try to speak, they don't understand me or they laugh at me and think I'm stupid. It has always been like this, but it still hurts.' Now read the verses again, and continue to imagine how he felt. There were people who cared enough to bring him to Jesus. Then there were many different ways Jesus showed his love as he took him on one side, touched his ears and his tongue, and prayed for him. Then he experienced a miracle of God's power at work. He could hear! He could speak! Jesus' command 'Be opened' were probably the first words he ever heard.

The story reminds me how I take for granted my ability to hear and to speak. I want to thank God today for my ears and my mouth and to pray for sensitivity towards those less fortunate. And if you are deaf or have an impediment in your speech, ask God for strength to live graciously with the hindrance and for patience with the rest of us when we are insensitive.

One more thought from today's story. In their excitement about the miracle the healed man and the bystanders chatted unrestrainedly about it. But Jesus had told them not to tell anyone; that leads me to pray:

Pray

*Lord, I pray that I may not be deaf to your voice. May I know when you want me to speak about you and when you want me to keep quiet.*

RG

Mark 8:22–26 (NIV)

# Love, wisdom and power

They came to Bethsaida, and some people brought a blind man and begged Jesus to touch him. He took the blind man by the hand and led him outside the village. When he had spat on the man's eyes and put his hands on him, Jesus asked, 'Do you see anything?' He looked up and said, 'I see people; they look like trees walking around.' Once more Jesus put his hands on the man's eyes. Then his eyes were opened, his sight was restored, and he saw everything clearly. Jesus sent him home, saying 'Don't go into the village.'

In the past two weeks, as we have read more of the narrative in St Mark's Gospel, we have seen Jesus' power in action in many ways; his power over nature, over chronic illness and physical handicap, over death, over evil spirits. We have seen his power released through people's faith or blocked through their disbelief. We have seen his power to give sight and hearing and to equip his followers for ministry, and his own need for power to be replenished by his Father. And we have seen a wide variety of response from those who met him; faith and trust; fear and astonishment; scepticism and doubt; outright disbelief and opposition.

Re-read today's story. I wonder what you particularly notice? Three things strike me. The first is the way the man's friends showed their concern for him. It challenges me to bring my friends to Jesus in prayer and beg for his help for them. Then Jesus sets me an example by his sensitive care for the man in the way he took him away

from the crowd, touched his eyes and asked him how they were. Finally, I see how the healing came in stages. When we ourselves pray for healing from any illness or impediment (for ourselves or for another person) we need to trust God both for his power and also for his wisdom, for whatever measure or means of healing he chooses. His agenda may be different from ours—but his is always right. Paul had some unknown affliction, and wrote 'Three times I pleaded with the Lord to take it away from me. But he said to me, 'My grace is sufficient for you, for my power is made perfect in weakness.'' (2 Corinthians 12:8–9)

A prayer

*Lord, you know all my situation. Please help me to trust your immeasurable power and your unfailing wisdom.*

RG

Luke 9:22–25 (NRSV)

# Winning by losing

[Jesus said], 'The Son of Man must undergo great suffering, and be rejected by the elders, chief priests and scribes, and be killed, and on the third day be raised.' Then he said to them all, 'If any want to become my followers, let them deny themselves and take up their cross daily and follow me. For those who want to save their life will lose it, and those who lose their life for my sake will save it. What does it profit them if they gain the whole world, but lose or forfeit themselves?'

The King James Version spoke in verse 24 of the person who lost his 'soul' while gaining the whole world. The word, in fact, as translated here and in all the modern versions, is 'himself'. The NIV has 'true self'. It doesn't mean 'self' in the sense of ME! It refers to that part of my being which expresses who I really am—the part of me that reflects my Creator's image, the part of me that will live on beyond death. So 'soul' wasn't a bad translation, even though the word itself isn't to be found here!

The challenge of this saying is particularly sharp for modern people, it would seem. We are bombarded with advice to 'do our own thing', to 'be our own person', to fight for our rights and assert our independence. And here is Jesus telling his followers that they should do exactly the opposite: deny themselves, take up a cross and follow the footsteps of one who lived not for himself but for others. It's a staggering contrast! And one has to say that it asks questions about any kind of 'Christianity' which seems to major on 'self-fulfilment', 'prosperity' or my own personal well-being. The Gospel is not there to make me 'happy' but to help me to be what God intends for me to be.

Of course, in following Jesus, as his first disciples found, there is great joy and fulfilment. Indeed, in the words of this passage, they will 'find themselves'. But the price is to let go of self, not to cling to it.

## A reflection

*Almighty God, whose most dear Son went not up to joy but first he suffered pain, and entered not into glory before he was crucified: mercifully grant that we, walking in the way of the cross, may find it none other than the way of life and peace; through Jesus Christ our Lord.*

Collect for Lent 3, ASB

DW

### Isaiah 40:1–5 (NRSV)

# A time for healing

Comfort, O comfort my people, says your God. Speak tenderly to Jerusalem, and cry to her that she has served her term, that her penalty is paid, that she has received from the Lord's hand double for all her sins. A voice cries out: 'In the wilderness prepare the way of the Lord, make straight in the desert a highway for our God. Every valley shall be lifted up, and every mountain and hill shall be made low; the uneven ground shall become level, and the rough places a plain. Then the glory of the Lord shall be revealed, and all people shall see it together, for the mouth of the Lord has spoken.'

These opening sentences of what we call Second Isaiah are among the most dramatic and thrilling in the Bible. The people of Judah and Jerusalem have sinned, and they have paid heavily for their sin. The Assyrians have conquered them. Tens of thousands have been taken away into captivity. There have been years of suffering and heartbreak, so awful that they must have thought that God had forgotten them. What made it even worse was the thought that it was all completely deserved—it was their own fault. They had ignored warning after warning. To suffer is bad enough, but to suffer when we know it's our own fault is almost unbearable.

But God hasn't forgotten them. He is a God of mercy. Yes, they had sinned, and the lesson had to be learned. But God doesn't bear grudges! And so the moment is coming, says the prophet, when God will decare that they've 'served their term' (rather like a convicted criminal in prison) and the time for their release has arrived. The 'voice' (of God, presumably) cries out: 'Prepare the way of the Lord!' When the conquering king's army marched in, he often created a new road for the purpose, a splendid 'triumphal way'—you can still see Roman ones in Italy. Well, the Lord's conquering army was coming, and a glorious triumphal way to be created. And when the road was ready the king would come!

It's not only the people of Judah long ago who need to know that God doesn't keep old scores. Sin repented is sin forgotten. Our past disobedience may have caused grievous pain, but it will come to an end, and when it does the king will return in all his glory.

### A reflection

*When I am tempted to think that my punishment will never end, remind me, Lord, that you don't hold grudges—perhaps all that you are waiting for is my true repentance?*

DW

Isaiah 40:6–8 (NRSV)

# The eternal Word

A voice says 'Cry out!' And I said, 'What shall I cry?' All people are grass, their constancy is like the flower of the field. The grass withers, the flower fades, when the breath of the Lord blows upon it; surely the people are grass. The grass withers, the flower fades; but the word of our God will stand forever.'

This passage is part of what seems to be a three-way dialogue between a heavenly 'voice', the 'word of the Lord', and the prophet. The 'voice' gives orders to the prophet: 'prepare the way' (v. 3), 'cry out' (v. 6). The Lord has a message of comfort and encouragement for the beleaguered people of Judah. And the prophet—we shall have to call him 'Second Isaiah'—tries to carry out the commands and convey the message. The message here is about the 'word of our God', which 'stands for ever', no matter how fickle and inconstant the people may be. They—and we, perhaps?—are about as reliable as the wild flowers in the fields around Jerusalem, which spring up in great abundance in April and are gone within a few weeks, victims of sun and wind. But their inconstancy does not affect God's reliability. If he makes a promise, he will keep it. His 'word' is his bond. This idea of the 'word of the Lord' runs right through the Scriptures, of course. It's probably most helpful to think of it as God's purpose revealed—what he wants us to know. His 'word' brought everything into being at the creation: he spoke ('Let there be light!') and it happened. His 'word' was revealed in the moral Law and in his covenant with Israel. It was revealed through the prophets, who could say, 'thus says the Lord'. And, most clearly of all, it was eventually revealed through his Son, Jesus: 'The Word was made flesh...'

We can also think of God's word as 'meaning' or 'explanation'. God has never wanted us to be in the dark about his purposes, so in different ways at different times he has made his meaning known. The people of Judah had been baffled that 'their' God had not acted to deliver them from oppression and enslavement. Now the 'meaning' was to become clear. The 'word of the Lord' which 'stands forever' is our guarantee that life is not without meaning, however baffling it may seem at the moment. God is utterly reliable.

### A reflection

*In a world of constant change and bewildering unreliability, help me to trust in the reliable and sure purposes of God, whose 'word... stands for ever'.*
DW

Isaiah 40:9–11 (NRSV)

# *Meekness and majesty*

'Get you up to a high mountain, O Zion, herald of good tidings; lift up your voice with strength, O Jerusalem, herald of good tidings, lift it up, do not fear; say to the cities of Judah, "Here is your God!" See, the Lord God comes with might, and his arm rules for him; his reward is with him, and his recompense before him. He will feed his flock like a shepherd; he will gather the lambs in his arms, and carry them in his bosom, and gently lead the mother sheep.'

The 'word' that God had for the people of Judah after their years of suffering is described here as 'good tidings'— 'good news'. The Lord God was coming: he was about to move to deliver them. The years of punishment were soon to be over and the time of deliverance or redemption was at hand.

But there was a deeper message than that in these verses, which tell the people what kind of a God was coming to deliver them. Certainly he is a God of power, more than strong enough to deal with their mighty enemies. His 'arm'—a symbol of strength—was able to ensure compliance with his will: it 'rules for him'. He may have withheld his power for a time, in line with his purposes, but nobody should assume from that that he was powerless—a mistake people have always made.

But he is also a 'shepherd', one of the great images of the good king in the life of Israel. A shepherd has to be strong, of course, to defend his charges—in those days, to fight off wild beasts, perhaps, or sheep-stealers. But he has to combine that with tenderness, gathering the tiny lambs in his arms and gently leading the ewes heavy with pregnancy.

It's sometimes quite hard to get the balance right in our understanding of who God is and what he can do. Some of us will tend to think of God in his majesty and power, inspiring awe and obedience. Others will prefer to experience God as the gentle Shepherd of his flock, guiding and caring for his people with tenderness and compassion. Both are true; both need to be experienced by the Christian. A God of power without love would be a tyrant (and some people, sadly, see him like that). A God of love without power would not be God at all..

A reflection

*Let us be grateful that our God combines in one person both infinite power and infinite love. Let us not forget that power, nor presume on that love.*

DW

Isaiah 40:21–24 (NRSV)

# The Ruler of the rulers

Have you not known? Have you not heard? Has it not been told you from the beginning? Have you not understood from the foundations of the earth? It is he who sits above the circle of the earth, and its inhabitants are like grasshoppers; who stretches out the heavens like a curtain, and spreads them like a tent to live in; who brings princes to naught, and makes the rulers of the earth as nothing. Scarcely are they planted, scarcely sown, scarcely has their stem taken root in the earth, when he blows upon them, and they wither, and the tempest carries them off like stubble.

This is a magnificent piece of Hebrew poetry, where the device of 'parallelism' is used to dramatic effect. Everything is said twice, but it isn't simply repetition: the parallel image always adds something, or extends the idea—'known... heard... told... understood...' The sky is a 'curtain' stretched out to cover the earth, but it's also a 'tent' under which its inhabitants can dwell.

The context is the preceding passage (vv. 12–20), which compares the glory, power and wisdom of God with his rivals: the idols of the heathen, made from wood or silver, or the rulers of the powerful nations of the ancient world. The people of Judah—God's people—have been attracted by the first and in awe of the second, yet in comparison with the awesome power of the Creator, what were they? The idols were man-made, no more than artifacts. And the princes of the nations were subject to God's rule and judgment, eventually, like all human flesh, to wither and die (v. 24).

Long, long ago, when I was a choirboy, I can remember being intrigued by the phrase in the 'old' Prayer Book which described God as 'the only ruler of princes'. It didn't mean much to me then (though I liked the sound of it!), but it must have meant a lot to people in Tudor England, whose lives were dictated by the whims of their 'princes'. One would tear down monasteries, another would burn 'heretics' at the stake. Their power must have seemed terrible. Yet ... God was the 'Ruler of princes'—the very point being made here by the prophet of Israel to a people similarly in awe of the power and authority of earthly rulers. Thank God for a King who rules with absolute justice and absolute compassion!

## A reflection

*Help me to understand who is really ruling the affairs of the world—its loving Creator.*

DW

Isaiah 40:28–31 (NRSV)

# *The giver of strength*

Have you not known? Have you not heard? The Lord is the ever-lasting God, the Creator of the ends of the earth. He does not faint or grow weary; his understanding is unsearchable. He gives power to the faint, and strengthens the powerless. Even youths will faint and be weary, and the young will fall exhausted; but those who wait for the Lord shall renew their strength, they shall mount up with wings like eagles, they shall run and not be weary, they shall walk and not faint.

This beautiful piece of poetry will encourage all of us who sometimes feel 'faint and weary'! It is actually the answer to the questions posed in verse 27, where the people of Israel and Judah are imagined as asking God why he has not stood up for their 'rights'—as though he lacked the power or strength to come to their help. The truth is precisely the opposite. Even the fittest and strongest of human beings eventually get tired and exhausted, but God 'does not faint or grow weary' (v. 28b).

But the marvellous news is even better than that! God not only has strength in himself, but he 'gives power to the faint and strengthens the powerless'. This gift, he says, is for those who 'wait for the Lord'—who are not impatient or demanding, but patiently trust in him. 'Waiting' sounds a rather passive occupation and the English word 'wait' is essentially neutral. But the Hebrew word is very positive. To wait is to expect, and that is often the most positive thing

that we can do. We may be tempted to struggle and fret when what God wants us to do is quietly trust him.

And when we do, according to the promise here, he will renew our strength—'recharge our batteries' might be a modern parallel! Far from remaining worn out, exhausted or powerless, we shall soar aloft like eagles, rising above our problems and difficulties. It's a marvellous picture and a tremendous encouragement when we feel 'down'. The strength of God can be transferred to us.

### A reflection

*'Waiting on God' is never the easy option, because it involves accepting that we cannot 'do it ourselves'. In moments of human weakness, when we feel tired, weary and even tempted to give up, the invitation is to 'wait for the Lord'. In his own time, he will show us how to draw strength from his own inexhaustible well.*

DW

## Luke 13:18–19; 17:5–6 (NRSV)

# *The seed that grows into a tree*

The Women's World Day of Prayer started very small and then grew. Mary Ellen James was the wife of a Presbyterian minister in Brooklyn New York and the mother of seven children. As she looked at the world round her she had a deep concern for the inhumane and poor quality of life that she saw. So she called the women of her church to set aside just one day for prayer for home missions 'where there shall be confession of individual and national sins with offerings that fitly express the contrition.' That was in 1887. Now the vision of that one woman has spread all over the world.

The seed has grown into a tree. Now over 127 countries participate in the movement. Each year Christian women in a different country are chosen to write the service, which is translated into over 1,000 languages. Through the Women's World Day of Prayer women are encouraged:

• to be aware of the whole world and no longer live in isolation

• to take up the burdens of other people and pray with and for them

• to become more aware of their talents and use them in the service of others

Every year there is a different theme. This year it is 'The seed that grows into a tree'.

Jesus said therefore, 'What is the kingdom of God like? And to what should I compare it? It is like a mustard seed that someone took and sowed in the garden; it grew and became a tree, and the birds of the air made nests in its branches.'...

The apostles said to the Lord, 'Increase our faith!' The Lord replied, 'If you had faith the size of a mustard seed, you could say to this mulberry tree, "Be uprooted and planted in the sea", and it would obey you.'

### Pray and reflect

*Read again the three things which the Women's World Day of Prayer encourages women to do. Reflect on them, whether you are a woman or a man. Then pray. Lord Jesus Christ, I want the seed of faith in me to grow into a tree. I want to make a real difference to the world and to the people in it. Open my eyes to see where people are hurting, and where there are things that need to be changed. Show me what I can do— and give me strength and wisdom to do it. Amen.*

SB

### Isaiah 41:8–10 (NRSV)

# *No need to fear*

But you, Israel, my servant, Jacob, whom I have chosen, the off-spring of Abraham, my friend; you whom I took from the ends of the earth, and called from its farthest corners, saying to you, 'You are my servant, I have chosen you and not cast you off'; do not fear, for I am with you, do not be afraid, for I am your God; I will strengthen you, I will help you, I will uphold you with my victori-ous right hand.

I've always thought that the emptiest advice you can give to anyone is 'Don't worry'. But I've done it, thousands of times. Someone's child is ill, or their husband is about to have an operation, or they're about to take an important exam. 'Don't worry!' we say, as though simply saying it will somehow take away that nagging fear that lies like a cold stone at the pit of their stomach. But in other circumstances, the words 'don't worry' can be very, very re-assuring. If the doctor says, 'Don't worry, we've got her on a drip now and she'll be all right'. Or the surgeon assures you that he's done this opera-tion many hundreds of times. Or your tutor says that there's nothing to worry about, you've done the work and all you've got to do is not panic... well, that's different! They have the right to tell you not to worry; and, more than that, they have the authority to counter the anxiety. It's not what is said, but who says it!

God has the right to tell his people not to be anxious. They are his 'chil-dren', descendants of the ones he chose long ago and to whom he made solemn and binding promises. More than that, he is with them now, on their side, involved in their 'case'. And he has the resources to do everything for them that is necessary: 'I am your God ... I will strengthen you with my victorious right hand'. He has the right to tell them not to worry and he has the authority to deal with the things that are causing their fear.

We too can have the same confi-dence, for didn't Jesus use very similar words? 'You are my friends.' His famil-iar greeting to his friends was simply 'shalom', peace. He has the right and the authority to give us his peace, the 'peace of the Lord'.

A reflection

*When I am anxious, may I turn to the One who has both the right and the authority to give me true and lasting peace.*

DW

Luke 9:32–36a (NRSV)

# Listen to him!

Now Peter and his companions were weighed down with sleep; but since they had stayed awake, they saw his glory and the two men who stood with him. Just as they were leaving him, Peter said to Jesus, 'Master, it is good for us to be here; let us make three dwellings, one for you, one for Moses and one for Elijah'—not knowing what he said. While he was saying this, a cloud came and overshadowed them; and they were terrified as they entered the cloud. Then from the cloud came a voice that said, 'This is my Son, my Chosen; listen to him!'

Here's a familiar human problem in a highly unfamiliar setting! It amounts to this: when we have a marvellous, 'mountain-top' experience, do we try to hold on to it, or do we learn from it and move on? In ordinary life it happens with special holidays—I know many people who have enjoyed a holiday so much that they've decided to move home to the area—only to find that rural Wales (for instance) is not quite the same in February as it is in the golden light of June! In spiritual experience, we can try to retain or repeat a wonderful moment of insight or blessing, desperately hanging on to the vision—which then fades or melts away through our fingers. Peter tried to do that. Confronted with a vision of Jesus in glory, with the great patriarchs Moses and Elijah, all he could blurt out was a suggestion that they should try to make the experience permanent—to trap the eternal on a Palestinian hill-side, complete with tents to sleep in!

Two things followed his nervous suggestion. The first was a 'cloud'—the great biblical symbol of the presence of God. This had been an experience that brought heaven to earth, as awesome as Sinai. The proper response was worship. The second was the voice of God from the cloud. His message was simple: understand what this experience means. This Jesus, your friend and teacher, is no other than my beloved and chosen Son. Don't build tents. Don't try to extend the visionary moment. Learn from it! Our experiences of God are to be part of a process of growth, through which we come to know him better. And nothing will help that progress more than 'listening to Jesus'.

## A reflection

*It is marvellous that sometimes we have memorable moments of blessing. They are to be remembered, treasured, cherished... and their lessons learnt.*

DW

### Isaiah 41:17–20 (NRSV)

# *Water in the desert*

When the poor and needy seek water and there is none, and their tongue is parched with thirst, I the Lord will answer them, I the God of Israel will not forsake them. I will open rivers on the bare heights, and fountains in the midst of the valleys; I will make the wilderness a pool of water, and the dry land springs of water. I will put in the wilderness the cedar, the acacia, the myrtle and the olive; I will set in the desert the cypress, the plane and the pine together, so that all may see and know, all may consider and understand, that the hand of the Lord has done this, the Holy One of Israel has created it.

The key to this passage is probably the word 'answer' in verse 17. Presumably the picture of a God who brings his people through the desert into a promised land is there to answer an objection from the fearful exiles, anxious about the rigours of the journey home in their state of poverty and weakness. They should not be fearful. Didn't God do all this and more for their forefathers in the desert, as Moses led them out of Egypt? Didn't God give them water and food, protection and shelter? God hasn't changed, and he will do the same for them.

The opening part of chapter 40 spoke of this coming homeward march. Now they are being reassured that God will be with them through its rigours, providing water in the wilderness and shade from trees that will miraculously spring up, providing ready-made oases on the journey. And this time God won't use an intermediary like Moses; he will care for them himself: 'understand that the hand of the Lord has done this'. The result of God's care for the returning exiles would be a universal recognition that the 'Holy One of Israel' is indeed God. The 'all' in verse 20 refers to the onlooking nations of unbelievers. God would do it for his own people, but through doing it all nations would be drawn to believe in him.

It is right and proper to trust that 'my God will fully satisfy every need of yours', as St Paul assured the Christians at Philippi. But in blessing his people he is working towards the blessing of the whole world.

### A reflection

*God will meet all our needs on our journey towards the 'Promised Land'— refreshment, protection, strength. May his generosity to us be reflected into the lives of those around us.*

DW

Isaiah 42: 1–4 (NRSV)

# The Servant of the Lord

Here is my servant, whom I uphold, my chosen, in whom my soul delights; I have put my spirit upon him; he will bring forth justice to the nations. He will not cry or lift up his voice, or make it heard in the street; a bruised reed he will not break, and a dimly burning wick he will not quench; he will faithfully bring forth justice. He will not grow faint or be crushed until he has established justice in the earth; and the coastlands wait for his teaching.

This is one of the 'Servant Songs' of Second Isaiah. Who is this 'servant'? Is he the prophet himself? Or Israel and Jacob (as some manuscripts suggest)? Or the future anointed king, the messiah? Probably all three! Prophecy is not a precise, scientific operation and neither is its interpretation. Isaiah may indeed have received these words as a prophetic promise, a kind of second commissioning, following all the opposition he had faced. But that doesn't mean that they can't have a wider meaning, involving all the servant-people of God then and now, and represented most perfectly by the Servant-Son himself, Jesus. After all, Matthew applies these very words to Jesus, and they seem very apt (Matthew 12:18–21).

There is also here a picture of the true Servant of God, which is surely applicable to all time. He is filled with the Spirit (v. 1), so that he is directed and empowered by God alone. He is concerned with justice for all ('the nations', not just Judah). He is not loud, aggressive or spectacular (v. 2),

but sets out to encourage those with a little faith and to affirm those whose faith is under attack ('bruised reeds' and 'dimly burning wicks'). The true Servant of God is more concerned to build up than to destroy.

And the true Servant is not easily discouraged. He (or she) knows that the task is enormous—to 'establish justice in the earth' and to proclaim the news of God to the 'coastlands' (a vague phrase meaning 'distant countries'). As we seek to do whatever God has called us to do, there will be times when it all seems too much and our hearts begin to fail. It is then that we need to remember whose servants we are, and whose Spirit has been put within us.

### A reflection

*As God's servant in small things, help me to model my life on the true Servant, his anointed Son, and gently, quietly and perseveringly to fulfill my calling.*

DW

### Isaiah 42:5–7 (NRSV)

# *Setting captives free*

Thus says God, the Lord, who created the heavens and stretched them out, who spread out the earth and what comes from it, who gives breath to the people upon it and spirit to those who walk in it: I am the Lord, I have called you in righteousness, I have taken you by the hand and kept you; I have given you as a covenant to the people, a light to the nations, to open the eyes that are blind, to bring out the prisoners from the dungeon, from the prison those who sit in darkness.

The 'you' in this passage is singular, so presumably refers to the Servant of the Lord, either the prophet or someone else who fulfils God's purposes. Some commentators have suggested that it may refer to the Persian king Cyrus, who released the captive Jews and allowed them to restore the temple in Jerusalem. What is obvious is that neither Cyrus nor, one would have thought, Isaiah himself could be described as a 'covenant to the people' or a 'light to the nations', so the complete fulfilment of this prophecy must await one who could be described in those terms. Not surprisingly, Christians have always seen the Messiah, Jesus, as the one who 'opened blind eyes', released prisoners from the slavery of sin, was the 'light for revelation to the Gentiles' (Luke 2:32) and the author of a new covenant.

There is really no conflict of interpretation here. Isaiah was God's servant, Israel/Judah was God's servant, and in the outworking of history even the pagan king Cyrus became God's servant. Jesus Christ was God's servant *par excellence*, so all the qualities we find spoken of here we should expect to see in perfection in Jesus. And so we do.

Probably of more immediate importance to us, we learn over and over again from these prophecies that God is concerned to set us free. Whatever our dungeons, whatever darkness circumstance or sin has cast around us, he sends his Servant to release us. And 'if the Son sets you free, you will be free indeed' (John 8:36). God is, and has always been, a God of freedom, the God of the passover and exodus, the God of the liberated slaves of Babylon.

### A reflection

*What holds me in? What constricts me, takes away my freedom? What is my own personal 'prison' or dungeon? God has given his Servant-Son the keys to the prison (Revelation 1:18) and he has come to set us free.*

DW

Isaiah 42:10–12 (NRSV)

# A new song

Sing to the Lord a new song, his praise from the end of the earth!
Let the sea roar and all that fills it, the coastlands and their inhabitants. Let the desert and its towns lift up their voice, the villages
that Kedar inhabits; let the inhabitants of Sela sing for joy, let
them shout from the tops of the mountains. Let them give glory to
the Lord, and declare his praise in the coastlands.

What does it mean to sing a 'new song'? For some people the mere mention of a 'new' hymn or song in church is enough to induce apoplexy! What most of us secretly prefer in worship is familiarity—C.S. Lewis once said that he could stand anything in church so long as it was 'familiar'. Yet time and again in the Psalms, and here in this prophetic song, God's people are exhorted, or even commanded, to sing a new song.

The 'new' song was not necessarily 'new' in the sense that it had never existed before, but that they had never experienced it in this way before. This 'song' reflected a new realization of God's goodness, mercy and grace—it came from renewed worshippers. Indeed, there seems to be little doubt that when we encounter God in a new way even 'old' songs become new!

This song would also be new because it would not just be sung inside the temple! It would sound forth from one end of the earth to the other. It would reach those distant 'coastlands'. It would be echoed in the Arabian desert ('Kedar') and in the rock city of Petra (the probable location of 'Sela'). The new song would reflect the glory of God into the whole world.

Of course, this hadn't yet happened. These prophetic songs in Second Isaiah are unique in that they celebrate not the past actions of the Lord but future ones. In other words, they are songs of faith, praise for something which hasn't happened yet but is confidently expected. In a very true sense, all our praise should reflect both thankfulness for the past and confident trust for the future. Those are the matching chords of the new song!

## A reflection

*May God give me this true spirit of
praise, so that with a renewed faith I
may sing the new song—in
thankfulness for the past and trust for
the future.*

DW

### Isaiah 42:18–20 (NRSV)

# *Servants who cannot see*

Listen, you that are deaf; and you that are blind, look up and see! Who is blind but my servant, or deaf like my messenger whom I send? Who is blind like my dedicated one, or blind like the servant of the Lord? He sees many things, but does not observe them; his ears are open, but he does not hear.

This is by any standards quite a difficult passage, but its basic message seems quite clear. We have already heard the exiles complaining that God is, at it were, blind to their fate (see, for example, 40:27). They feel that he has shut his eyes and closed his ears to their suffering. But God's riposte is blunt: 'It's not I who am blind, but you!' You have failed to see that it's your sins and disobedience that have caused all this, with the result that I, the Lord, have a 'messenger' (Israel) who is deaf to my word and a servant-nation that is blind to my will. This makes God's promises of deliverance all the more generous, of course.

The wider application is challenging. Modern Christians tend to spend a good deal of time either complaining ('Why does God let this happen?') or trying to defend their God against the complaints of others, as though it is God who is under judgment. But the truth is that it is we who are under judgment. It is our eyes that are blind to the truth of our condition. It is human sin, not God's failure, that has brought about our plight. To put it crudely, by and large we are villains, not victims!

And the situation is made worse by the fact that we believe we can see everything! As the old saying goes, 'There's none so blind as those who won't see'. When things go wrong, our first instinct isn't to ask 'Is there something in me, in my life or behaviour, that has contributed to this?' Instead, we tend to ask, 'Why has God done this to me?' The result is that we render ourselves deaf and blind to whatever God is saying to us in the situation. 'It's all his fault; let him sort it out!'

That was precisely the attitude of the people of Judah in Isaiah's day. They were called to be God's messengers, but they'd completely failed to grasp the message themselves!

---

### A reflection

*There are two great truths here. The first is that we need to understand the true cause of our situation and our own contribution to it. The second is that our present situation is no reason for doubting that God is working for our ultimate good.*

DW

### Isaiah 43:1–3a (NRSV)

# 'You are mine'

But now thus says the Lord, he who created you, O Jacob, he who formed you, O Israel: Do not fear, for I have redeemed you; I have called you by name, you are mine. When you pass through the waters, I will be with you; and through the rivers, they shall not overwhelm you; when you walk through fire you shall not be burned, and the flame shall not consume you. For I am the Lord your God, the Holy One of Israel, your Saviour.

This passage describes God's relationship to his people in terms of intimacy and kinship. He created and formed them (the verbs are the same as those used of the creation of the world). They belong to him. He has named them (like a parent naming a child). Most strikingly of all, he has 'redeemed' them. When they go through times of trial he will be with them.

Second Isaiah likes to describe God as the 'redeemer' of his people—the Hebrew word is go'el. It refers to the 'near kinsman' who was obliged to come to the help of his family members when they were in trouble. The most specific instance of this was when they fell into slavery. The go'el was expected—actually required—to pay for their freedom. It was in that sense that he was their 'redeemer': he paid the price of their freedom (see Leviticus 25:47–49).

The prophet likens God, time and again, to that 'near kinsman', who has put himself under an obligation to pay the price of their freedom. He had done it in the past (from slavery in Egypt) and he would do it again. By his very nature, and by promise, God is the 'redeemer' of his people, committed to come to their help.

At the same time, this 'near kinsman', who acts in such an intimate and familiar way on their behalf, is still 'the Lord your God, the Holy One of Israel'. The two roles were complementary, not contradictory. God was their Saviour and their Lord.

This is something Christians should be able to see expressed in their own understanding of Jesus. He also calls his disciples 'his own', his 'little ones'. They are his 'friends', children of his Father. He pays the price of their freedom with his own life. He commits himself to come to our help. But he is also, and always, 'Lord of all'.

---

### A reflection

*When I am called to pass through times of trouble—the waters of suffering, the fire of pain or disappointment—may I know that my kinsman-redeemer is 'with me'.*

DW

### John 12:23–28 (NRSV)

# *Glorified through suffering*

Jesus answered them, 'The hour has come for the Son of Man to be glorified. Very truly, I tell you, unless a grain of wheat falls into the earth and dies, it remains just a single grain; but if it dies, it bears much fruit. Those who love their life lose it, and those who hate their life in this world will keep it for eternal life. Whoever serves me must follow me, and where I am, there my servant will be also. Whoever serves me, the Father will honour. Now my soul is troubled. And what should I say—"Father, save me from this hour"? No, it is for this reason that I have come to this hour.'

The theme of the readings in many churches on this fifth Sunday in Lent is the Cross, and here we see Jesus himself 'troubled' by some of the issues it raises. He is on the brink of his great suffering on the cross, by which, in the unique vocabulary of John's Gospel, he and the Father will be 'glorified'. But there's nothing 'glorious' about crucifixion, probably the cruellest and most inhumane method of execution ever employed by the ever-ingenious human race. There's no dignity in slow dislocation of joints and organs; nothing splendid or heroic about hanging in the hot sun for hour after hour until pain finally ends in a red mist of oblivion.

Jesus the man was appalled at the prospect. That, for me, is the message of Gethsemane in the synoptic Gospels (Matthew, Mark and Luke) and his anguished questioning here. Could he ask God to spare him the suffering? He knew the answer, of course. No, because all he had come to do was to be summed up in that act of self-sacrifice. Unless the 'grain of wheat' fell to the ground and died, the rich harvest of eternal life would never be reaped. What Jesus accepted here was the purpose: his suffering was not meaningless.

But sometimes human suffering does seem meaningless—the death of a child, the murder of a young girl, the slow decline of a person with an incurable condition. Is there any 'glory' there, any 'harvest' to be reaped? Well, Jesus said 'Whoever serves me must follow me', and that doesn't only mean to the places of comfort and prosperity. When his servant walks the way of the cross, Jesus has been there first. Perhaps only those who suffer can ever know what it is fully to follow him, and to be 'honoured' by their heavenly Father (v. 26).

### A reflection

*Whoever serves must follow Jesus, even to a cross. Whoever follows, the Father will honour.*

DW

## Isaiah 43:16–19 (NRSV)

# A way through the waters

**Thus says the Lord, who makes a way in the sea, a path in the mighty waters, who brings out chariot and horse, army and warrior; they lie down, they cannot rise, they are extinguished, quenched like a wick: Do not remember the former things, or consider things of old. I am about to do a new thing; now it springs forth, do you not perceive? I will make a way in the wilderness and rivers in the desert.**

Not for the first time, a Jewish hymn of salvation is built around the familiar images of the exodus from Egypt under Moses—the echoes of Exodus 14 are unmistakeable. It's as though the prophet is reminding the doubters among the Jews that what God has done in the past he can do again. Military might and logistical problems—armies and warriors, seas and 'mighty waters'—are no problem to him.

But if he is 'reminding' them, why does he say 'do not remember' ... 'do not consider things of old'? Surely he wanted them to remember, and to renew their faith and hope by the memory of God's past power and salvation? Well, yes, of course he did, and the words here must be rhetorical. Often the prophet urges them to remember (see, for example, 46:9). But now, he suggests, God is going to do such a wonderful thing that even the exodus from Egypt will pale into insignificance beside it. They're about to receive a new set of 'memories'!

God is about to do a 'new thing'.

Indeed, 'now it springs forth'—it is at hand. This 'new thing' is a reminder that God doesn't just repeat himself. He is the true 'original'! On this occasion the 'new thing' would be a new way through the wilderness, back from captivity. But more than that, there would be 'rivers in the desert'—a picture of what had been barren and unproductive becoming green and fertile.

For us, this is a reminder of the ultimate promise of God, that he will make 'everything new' (Revelation 21:5). God is a God of change, of transformation and renewal. Those who insist on seeing their faith in God as a bulwark against change must face the fact that the Creator has never stopped creating!

### A reflection

*God has done marvellous things in the past, but he is the God of the present and the future as well. Truly, he is the 'God of surprises'.*

DW

Isaiah 44:1–5 (NRSV)

# *Water on a thirsty land*

But now hear, O Jacob my servant, Israel whom I have chosen! Thus says the Lord who made you, who formed you in the womb and will help you: Do not fear, O Jacob my servant, Jeshurun whom I have chosen. For I will pour water on the thirsty land, and streams on the dry ground; I will pour my spirit upon your descendants, and my blessing on your offspring. They shall spring up like a green tamarisk, like willows by flowing streams. This one will say, 'I am the Lord's,' another will be called by the name of Jacob, yet another will write on the hand, 'The Lord's,' and adopt the name of Israel.

This is one of a number of 'oracles' in Second Isaiah built around the call, 'Fear not!' People are always saying, 'Don't worry!' but that's not a lot of help if the cause of the worry is still there. In this case, the Lord gives his people convincing evidence as to why they have no need to worry. They are his 'servants'; he has 'chosen' them; he has a purpose for their life, which he created from the very beginning ('in the womb'); he will 'help' them.

The oracle goes on to relate other ways in which the Lord would counter some of the common anxieties of the ancient (and often the modern) world. He would water their land and make it fertile, so they would not be victims of famine. And their children and grand-children would be blessed—they would be numerous (a great sign of blessing in Israel) and would flourish.

There is one more promise, contained in that rather obscure last verse. 'This one', 'another' and 'yet another' almost certainly refer not to members of Israel, God's already-chosen people, but to the people of the heathen lands around them. Seeing God's wonderful blessing on Israel, and their quiet confidence in him, the unbelievers and seekers would turn to the Lord, adopting his name, even (presumably metaphorically) writing it on their hands. There is no more effective way to draw others to the love of God than to experience it ourselves, and let his peace rule in our hearts. In a world of fear, it would be the confidence of those who trusted in the Lord that would attract people to him.

## A reflection

*'Perfect love casts out fear' (1 John 4:18). It is when people see that this has happened for us that they will also be drawn to the One who says 'Fear not!'—and deals with our fears in love.*

DW

## Isaiah 44:24–26a (NRSV)

# Trust my words

**Thus says the Lord, your redeemer, who formed you in the womb: I am the Lord, who made all things, who alone stretched out the heavens, who by myself spread out the earth; who frustrates the omens of liars, and makes fools of diviners; who turns back the wise, and makes their knowledge foolish; who confirms the word of his servant, and fulfils the prediction of his messengers.**

This passage is what the experts call a 'message formula'—it authenticates the message which God is giving through human mouths. In this case, it has a very specific purpose, but to find it you have to read on as far as verse 28. There, God says through his servant that 'Cyrus ...is my shepherd, and he shall carry out all my purpose'. And who is this Cyrus, who is to be God's agent for the rebuilding of the Jerusalem and the temple (v. 28), whom God calls his 'anointed one' (45:1)? None other than the heathen king of Persia!

No wonder the Lord is at pains to emphasize that the shocking message they are hearing from the prophet is nothing less than the truth. The One who created everything, who makes fools of the soothsayers and astrologers and makes the 'wise' look foolish, is assuring them that, unlikely and humiliating as it may seem to them, he is able to use a heathen king as the agent of his purposes—especially when the 'chosen ones' have failed so dismally.

It's worth thinking of the signifi-cance of this in our everyday experience of God. We do tend to put him in little boxes, to assume that God must always and exclusively work with the people we approve of, and in ways we recognize. Most of us can recall moments of shock when we have discovered that God has spoken to us through someone whose beliefs and opinions we have hitherto despised or deemed 'unsound' or unhelpful. In fact, God has a way of keeping us humble by ensuring that our little approved categories are highly provisional. At this moment, God may be speaking to us through the words or actions of an 'unbeliever', but we are deaf or blind to it because he is not 'one of us' (see Luke 9:49). God's truth is greater than its messengers.

---

### A reflection

*Help me to recognize when you are speaking to me, Lord: through the Bible, yes, but also through even unlikely people and events.*

DW

# *Every corner of the earth*

Turn to me and be saved, all the ends of the earth! For I am God, and there is no other. By myself I have sworn, from my mouth has gone forth in righteousness a word that shall not return: 'To me every knee shall bow, every tongue shall swear.' Only in the Lord, it shall be said of me, are righteousness and strength; all who were incensed against him shall come to him and be ashamed. In the Lord all the offspring of Israel shall triumph and glory.

There are, as so often, two levels at which we can understand these words. As they were originally spoken, they were a message of encouragement to the exiled people of Judah-Israel. God had promised that he would deliver them from the hands of their enemies, and he would do it. More than that, the whole world would have to recognize it. To the great satisfaction of the erstwhile slaves, their erstwhile conquerors would have to grovel on bended knee before the God of Israel and swear their allegiance to him.

That is the only possible meaning of the prophecy as it was originally given and received. But Christians have always believed that beyond the immediate meaning of the words lies a deeper one, that could only be fulfilled when the true 'Servant of the Lord' appeared. So, in my view absolutely rightly, they saw in the great prophecies of second Isaiah splendid and inspiring pictures of the coming Messiah, Jesus, and of the even greater deliverance that God would bring to his people of the New Covenant. It is

unlikely, to say the least, that the prophet was looking on to a day when people from the 'ends of the earth' would turn to God and be saved, in the sense in which Christians would understand those words. He probably saw this promise simply as a demonstration of God's unique power. But Jesus the Messiah sent his followers with his message to 'all the nations' and St Paul tells us that one day 'every knee shall bow and every tongue confess that Jesus Christ is Lord' (Philippians 2:10)—a precise echo of the words here. Incidentally, what clearer evidence can there be of the apostle's belief in the divinity of Jesus than the transfer of this ancient promise from the Father to the Son?

### A reflection

*'Only in the Lord... are righteousness and strength.' There may be many paths to him, but he is the only source of true holiness and lasting strength.*
DW

### Isaiah 46:3–4 (NRSV)

# *When I am old and grey*

Listen to me, O house of Jacob, all the remnant of the house of Israel, who have been borne by me from your birth, carried from the womb; even to your old age I am he, even when you turn grey I will carry you. I have made, and I will bear; I will carry and will save.

'Will you still need me, will you still feed me, when I'm sixty-four?' The Beatles asked the question (in the days when, for me, sixty-four seemed a long way away and very old!). They wanted to know if love could survive old age. I suppose it's typical of the fickleness of youth that they couldn't understand that real love has nothing to do with the presence or absence of wrinkles, or with years on the calendar. True love doesn't change. As Shakespeare wrote, 'Love's not time's fool, though rosy lips within his bending sickle's compass come. Love alters not, but bears it out, even to the edge of Doom'. St Paul put it more succinctly: 'Love never ends' (1 Corinthians 13:8).

What is true of human love at its best is, of course, supremely true of God's love. Like a mother, he carries us from the womb. As our Creator, he has a stake in our destiny. In these words to Israel he is speaking of his original call, when he chose them out of all the nations of the earth. But the heart of his commitment to them is his covenant promise. God keeps his word, whatever the cost. Those he loves he loves to the end.

And so it is for us, because God's character doesn't change. He remains our faithful Creator, Father and God. The passage of the years may make enormous differences to us in many ways, but they make no difference at all to him. We change, but he remains the same and his love is utterly reliable and faithful. Indeed, the more we are conscious of our need of him, the more he will 'carry' us. 'Even to your old age . . . even when you turn grey' the One who has guarded us from the womb will continue to bear us up. That's a promise to cherish when the limbs are aching, the eyes are tired and the memory begins to falter!

### A reflection

*'Love never ends'—least of all God's love, which is reliable, faithful and true. As things change, and we change, we can put our trust in God's eternal changelessness.*

DW

Isaiah 47:12–15 (NRSV)

# No warmth at this fire!

Stand fast in your enchantments and your many sorceries, with which you have laboured from your youth; perhaps you may be able to succeed, perhaps you may inspire terror. You are wearied with your many consultations; let those who study the heavens stand up and save you, those who gaze at the stars, and at each new moon predict what shall befall you. See, they are like stubble, the fire consumes them; they cannot deliver themselves from the power of the flame. No coal for warming oneself is this, no fire to sit before! Such to you are those with whom you have laboured, who have trafficked with you from your youth; they all wander about in their own paths; there is no one to save you.

One of the great delusions of modern times is that we are a more rational and scientific people than our ignorant forefathers. How that can be sustained in a society so pre-occupied with superstition and astrology I can't imagine! It constantly amazes me how many apparently well-educated and rational people actually take note of the ludicrous predictions of the newspaper astrologers, as though our lives could possibly be shaped by the movements of planets. This passage—a savage satire on the Babylonian astrologers and soothsayers—may help to make it clear that God's people are to have no truck with this dangerous and misleading nonsense. It is not just 'harmless fun', for it implies that our destinies are in the hands of a power other than that of a loving and wise Creator-God.

It also offers empty comfort. In the prophet's ironic words, 'No coal for warming oneself is this'. The astrologers cannot even deliver themselves from destruction—Babylon was doomed because of its sins, and no amount of appealing to stars or planets would save it. There is a more general warning here, as relevant today as then: we are each of us responsible to God for our actions—and our destiny depends on our response to him, not to astrological predictions. God alone knows the future, which in his mercy he normally hides from us. We are to live, as the song says, 'one day at a time'. 'So do not worry about tomorrow,' said Jesus. 'Tomorrow will bring worries of its own.' What we pray for is grace for each day.

## A reflection

*What God alone knows, God alone can reveal. My future is in his hands, not the movement of planets.*

DW

Mark 11:8–10 (NJB)

# *The king they crucify*

Many people spread their cloaks on the road, and others greenery which they had cut in the fields. And those who went in front and those who followed were all shouting, 'Hosanna! Blessed is he who is coming in the name of the Lord! Blessed is the coming kingdom of David our father! Hosanna in the highest heavens!' He entered Jerusalem and went into the Temple.

The climax of Jesus' ministry begins. He had come to declare the kingdom of God. In Galilee he had fulfilled this by his teaching, continually urging a deeper understanding of God's law. He cut through the web of complications and conditions which had progressively enabled people to avoid its full demands and the direct service of God. Now he comes to Jerusalem, where the same logic of God's kingship will demand that he show, by his demonstration in the temple, how far Judaism had strayed from God's purposes—a demonstration which, not surprisingly, convinced the temple authorities that he must be put out of the way. At this stage, however, the people are shown as seeing Jesus' entry into Jerusalem as the declaration of God's kingship. They welcome in his person God's presence and power among them.

Lord Jesus, you bring among us the kingdom of your Father. As a Christian I acknowledge your Father's reign and that you are his messenger, our way to the Father and to membership of his kingdom. As a Bible-reader I seek to appreciate what you showed us by your life and teaching. I try to enter more closely into your reign, to submit my life more fully to your kingship. And yet do I really allow you to change my life? The chants of the people of Jerusalem were superficial and easy enough. They hailed you and the coming kingdom of David our father. But when you were standing trial no voice was raised to support you. Is my Christianity the same? I call upon you, claim to try to do your will. But when the trappings and promises of Christianity are inconvenient, do I brush you into a corner? Do I really forgive those who offend and upset me? Do I really love and seek the interests of those I dislike?

### A prayer

*Lord, during this Holy Week deepen my prayers, so that they are not just windy sayings but bonds of love, strongly forged, for your kingship.*

HW

## Mark 12:1–8 (NJB)

# *The son they kill*

He went on to speak to them in parables, 'A man planted a vineyard; he fenced it round, dug out a trough for the winepress and built a tower; then he leased it to tenants and went abroad. When the time came he sent a servant to his tenants to collect from them his share of the produce of the vineyard. But they seized the man, thrashed him and sent him away empty-handed... He sent another, and him they killed; then a number of others, and they thrashed some and killed the rest. He had still someone left: his beloved son. He sent him to them last of all, thinking, 'They will respect my son.' But... they seized him and killed him and threw him out of the vineyard.'

In the build-up to the arrest of Jesus this story must have played an important part. Jesus took the lovely poem in Isaiah about the vineyard of the beloved and turned it against the current custodians of the vineyard. They took it as personal criticism (as indeed it must have been meant) and refused to accept it. It was all of a piece with the outrageous behaviour of the Galilean preacher in the temple, a sort of verbal interpretation of what his action meant. This violent demonstration must have been puzzling, because he claimed the same authority as that of John the Baptist. The people remembered John, despite his nasty end, and enough had encountered him at the Jordan crossing to leave his memory fresh and revered. Were they still waiting for the coming of the kingship for which his washing in the Jordan had prepared them?

There may have been a vague unease among the leaders, but they successfully quieted their consciences and managed to blind themselves to inconvenient truths. Don't we all? It is really too inconvenient to take the Christian message seriously in all its implications. In our own way we are all selective, strident about some aspects, stealthily silent about others.

### A prayer

*Lord Jesus, as we come to the moment of your Passion and Resurrection, help me to be more objective about myself, to see in myself the faults which others see in me and you yourself pardon in me. In humility and helplessness I offer them to you to be redeemed by your love.*

HW

### Mark 14:3–7 (NJB)

# *Waste or worship?*

He was at Bethany in the house of Simon… at table when a woman came in with an alabaster jar of very costly ointment, pure nard. She broke the jar and poured the ointment on his head. Some who were there said to one another indignantly, 'Why this waste of ointment? Ointment like this could have been sold for over three hundred denarii and the money given to the poor'; and they were angry with her. But Jesus said, 'Leave her alone. Why are you upsetting her? What she had done for me is a good work. You have the poor with you always, and you can be kind to them whenever you wish, but you will not always have me.'

This anointing of Jesus at Bethany is the immediate prelude to his arrest and execution. Mark points this up for his readers by sandwiching it between the determination of the chief priests to liquidate Jesus and Judas' offer to betray him for money. The woman is lavish in her gesture: the jar itself is broken, so that there is no possibility of saving any of the ointment. The cost of it was a full year's wages for an agricultural labourer. It is an illogical gesture, one of love and devotion. (What good can flowers do to the dead? Yet we give them willingly as a sign of our own love and respect). Logic and practicalities have their limits. The woman's gesture and the disciples' complaint spark off the repeated debate about spending on churches and their embellishment. What are the relative claims of showing our loyalty and affection by making a noble 'home' for the Lord and of bringing relief and comfort to those whom he loves?

Besides an anointing of Jesus' body for burial, the gesture has a further significance: it is now, at the Passion, that his own kingship is to be made known. He is mocked as king of the Jews, and he reigns from the cross. So this is also a royal anointing.

### A prayer

*Lord, grant me to see your image in the poor, but nourish also my personal devotion and reckless love for you.*

HW

## Mark 14:17–20 (NJB)

# *He betrayed his friend*

When evening came he arrived with the Twelve. And while they were at table eating, Jesus said, 'In truth I tell you, one of you is about to betray me, one of you eating with me.' They were distressed and said to him, one after another, 'Not me, surely?' He said to them, 'It is one of the Twelve, one who is dipping into the same dish with me.'

Matthew's account of this incident is slightly different from Mark's, concentrating on the identification of the traitor. Mark brings out the treachery of his action in betraying the Master. To share a meal, the means of life, with someone is a sign of sharing that person's life. It is also a sign of the obvious cheerfulness of companionship. To share the same dish is more pointed still, especially as Judas is one of the small group of specially chosen companions.

Why did he desert and betray his leader? Some have suggested that it was simply the lure of money. Others have pointed to his nationalist name (a previous Judas had led the Maccabean revolt against the Syrian domination); they guess that Judas abandoned Jesus as soon as he saw that Jesus was no nationalist messiah, set to free the Jews from Roman rule.

The story of Judas' suicide by hanging also stresses his treachery. Suicide was almost unprecedented in the Bible. The one notable exception is that of Ahithophel, King David's companion and advisor, who betrayed his master and then hanged himself. Like other examples of such a tragic death, it must surely be the expression of total bewilderment and inability to see a way out of the situation, in Judas' case a realization that he could now do nothing to remedy his previous action, a sort of violent protest against, and self-alienation from what he himself had done.

This is only the beginning of the story of betrayal: as we go through the account of Jesus' passion we find each of his chosen disciples fleeing and leaving their Master to suffer unsupported. Peter has the courage to follow for a time, but then falls all the harder by denying his Master with curses and oaths.

---

A prayer

*Lord, grant me loyalty to my principles, even when it costs. Especially grant me loyalty to you in all things.*

HW

John 13:2–5, 12–15 (NJB)

# *The servant God*

They were at supper and the devil had already put it into the mind of Judas Iscariot son of Simon to betray him. Jesus knew that the Father had put everything into his hands, and that he had come from God and was returning to God, and he got up from table, removed his outer garments and, taking a towel, wrapped it round his waist; he then poured water into a basin and began to wash the disciples' feet and to wipe them with the towel he was wearing... When he had washed their feet and put on his outer garments again he went back to the table. 'Do you understand,' he said, 'what I have done to you? You call me Master and Lord, and rightly; so I am. If I, then, the Lord and Master, have washed your feet, you must wash each other's feet. I have given you an example so that you may copy what I have done to you.'

On this day of the Lord's Supper we have to choose from two possible readings: should it be this acted parable of Jesus' task of service, or should it be the institution of the eucharist? That too has the overtones of service, for Jesus is looking ahead to his act of sacrifice, his blood 'poured out for many'—as he quotes in allusion to the poem of the Suffering Servant of the Lord in Isaiah. Either way, the last supper was the pre-enactment beforehand of his passion, as the Christian eucharist is its re-enactment afterwards.

How much did Jesus know, at this last supper with his disciples, about the turn events were to take? On the merely human level he must have known that the temple authorities would never let him get away with the demonstration he had made in the temple. He had declared that the temple and the Judaism of which it was the centre were bankrupt. They could never afford to risk another such scene during the Passover festival, thronged as it was with zealous pilgrims from all the world. Yet calmly before the blow is struck he shows his resolution to serve his brethren.

### A prayer

*Lord Jesus, grant me to respond to your love, your affectionate care for me. Greater love has no man than this, to lay down his life for his friends.*
HW

## John 19:25–30 (NJB)

# *He died—for us*

Near the cross of Jesus stood his mother and his mother's sister... Seeing his mother and the disciple whom he loved standing near her, Jesus said to his mother, 'Woman, this is your son.' Then to the disciple he said, 'This is your mother.' And from that hour the disciple took her into his home. After this, Jesus knew that everything had now been completed and... he said, 'I am thirsty'. A jar full of sour wine stood there; so, putting a sponge soaked in the wine on a hyssop stick, they held it up to his mouth. After Jesus had taken the wine he said, 'It is fulfilled'; and bowing his head he gave up his spirit.

Rather than the gruesome details of that shameful execution, the evangelists paints a picture of Jesus' inner peace and control. He had come willingly and knowingly to this hour and he makes his final dispositions before leaving this world. Firstly he prepares the community which is to follow him. He joins together his mother, the first to receive him, with the Beloved Disciple. It is deliberate that the evangelist never tells us the name of this disciple, for—whoever he was—he stands for any disciple whom Jesus loves, the unnamed and universal disciple. Thus the little society, the nucleus of the Church, is formed at the foot of the cross, and shares in Jesus' supreme act of love.

Next the evangelist notes that even the last moment of Jesus' crucifixion, his thirst, fulfills the scripture. It was the scriptures which showed the will of God. This is a final indication, then, that it was God's plan that his Son should die this death.

Finally, and only when he has accepted the moment, Jesus bows his head. This is not the end but the beginning. With one of those mysterious Johannine double-meanings the evangelist tells us that this is the moment when the Spirit is given. This Spirit of Jesus will empower the Church and be with his disciples until the end of time. It makes Jesus present even when he appears to be absent.

### A prayer

*Lord Jesus, you did not leave your followers orphans, but prepared the loving family which was to be enlivened by your Spirit. Make me the willing instrument of your Spirit, joined to you in all things, even your suffering.*

HW

John 19:31–34, 40–42 (NJB)

# *Wait*

It was the Day of Preparation, and to avoid the bodies' remaining on the cross during the Sabbath—since that Sabbath was a day of special solemnity—the Jews asked Pilate to have the legs broken and the bodies taken away... When they came to Jesus, they saw he was already dead, and so one of the soldiers pierced his side with a lance, and immediately there came out blood and water... They took the body of Jesus and bound it in linen cloths with the spices, following the Jewish burial custom. At the place where he had been crucified there was a garden, and in this garden a new tomb in which no one had yet been buried. Since it was the Jewish Day of Preparation and the tomb was nearby, they laid Jesus there.

There is a certain finality about the account of the burial of Jesus. It seems the end of the story. This gives to Holy Saturday a sense of repose, not of hopelessness but of suspended animation. It is as though the day comes between one life and another, yet more wonderful life. There is a sense of breathless expectancy as the world waits for the new life to be revealed.

The ancient Christian tradition is that at this moment Christ descended to the underworld to draw up into his risen company the patriarchs who had longed for his day and not seen it. Matthew already pictures the dead rising from their tombs and going into the holy city at the moment of Christ's death and of the rending of the veil of the temple. The same is commemorated in the wonderful Byzantine mosaics of Christ grasping Adam by the wrist to draw him from the tomb. Adam symbolizes all the dead who have not known Christ, who yet are saved by him—a far greater crowd than any Byzantines ever envisaged. The rejoicing of countless millions of the human race is about to begin!

So for the Christian on this earth Holy Saturday is a day of quiet waiting, poised between Good Friday and Easter Sunday, a day to reflect on the evil that is past and the good which must yet come to birth.

A prayer

*Lord Jesus, as we commemorate your repose in death, grant me to appreciate a real sense of loss, and sense of what life would be without you.*

HW

## Mark 16:2–8 (NJB)

# *He has risen!*

Very early in the morning on the first day of the week [Mary of Magdala, Mary the mother of James, and Salome] went to the tomb when the sun had risen. They had been saying to one another, 'Who will roll away the stone for us from the entrance to the tomb?' But when they looked they saw that the stone—which was very big—had already been rolled back. On entering the tomb they saw a young man in a white robe seated on the right-hand side, and they were struck with amazement. But he said to them, 'There is no need to be so amazed. You are looking for Jesus of Nazareth, who was crucified: he has risen, he is not here'... And the women came out and ran away from the tomb because they were frightened out of their wits; and they said nothing to anyone, for they were afraid.

The dominant note of this earliest account of the finding of the empty tomb is fear, reverence and amazement. The women are so thrown off balance, so scared that they do not even check whether the tomb is in fact empty. Why were they so terrified? Every Jew (with the possible exception of the Sadducees) knew that all would rise again at the last day, and here the resurrection had actually happened! Did this mean that the last day had come? Had the great Day of the Lord arrived? Was this the end of time? Such thoughts must have whirled through their heads, and duly terrified them.

What message for us has their experience, so dramatically told by the evangelist? With the resurrection of Christ the Day of the Lord did, in some sense, occur. God entered history in a new way and brought a new phase of history into being. Now, in raising Christ from death, God had changed the very conditions of being. Death, which used to be so final, is no longer the bitter end of things. God had taken fully to himself one member of the human race, and so accomplished the union of God and humanity which was the goal of history. Jesus' entry into the divine glory gives us new hope, new assurance of our own goal.

### A prayer

*On this Day of the Resurrection grant my prayer, Lord, that I may so put my trust in you that I may join your Son Jesus in your glory.*

HW

## Colossians 3:1–4 (NJB)

# *A prayer to the Christ who died and is alive*

Since you have been raised up to be with Christ, you must look for the things that are above, where Christ is, sitting at God's right hand. Let your thoughts be on things above, not on the things that are on the earth, because you have died, and now the life you have is hidden with Christ in God. But when Christ is revealed— and he is your life—you, too, will be revealed with him in glory.

Lord Jesus, by baptism I have become immersed into your death so that I may share with you your risen glory. I have become part of your Body. My life is no longer mine but yours, my fingers are your fingers, my breath is your breath, your history is my history. I have committed myself to you, and you have taken me to yourself. I have been buried with Christ. I share Christ's inheritance. I am one body with Christ.

But though I live with your breath, your Spirit, I know only too well that my old self is still at work. The good I want to do, I cannot do; the evil which I do not want is what I do. I have yet to be fully transformed into you. It is still in the future that I will be glorified with Christ, that I will be seated with Christ at God's right hand. Life is a mass of cares, joys, preoccupations and plans, bravery and bitchiness, jealousies and generosity. I need your help to keep my thoughts on things above. My life is indeed *hidden* with you in God, and sometimes so well hidden that I cannot perceive it. If I am to be revealed with you in glory, prepare me now, by bringing me closer to you, by keeping me faithful to your ways. Let my peace be in you, my joy be in you. Bring me to act as a member of your Body, as a part of your being. Perhaps even permit me to share your suffering, since you suffered in order to be glorified— but only so far as you give me strength to rejoice in you as well.

*HW*

## John 20:19–22 (NJB)

# The giving of the Holy Spirit

The doors were closed in the room where the disciples were, for fear of the Jews. Jesus came and stood among them. He said to them, 'Peace be with you... As the Father sent me, so am I sending you.' After saying this he breathed on them and said, 'Receive the Holy Spirit.'

This blessing by the risen Christ really constitutes the foundation of the Christian community or Church. It has all the elements of the essence of the Church. First, he blesses his followers with peace. 'Peace' or 'Shalom' was and remains a traditional Jewish blessing, but in Christian usage it comes to stand especially for the messianic peace which Christ brings. It is part of the greeting at the beginning of each of Paul's letters, and the Good News is referred to simply as 'the gospel of peace'. This peace is not simply absence of strife, but a positive bond of tranquillity between those who in harmony strive together to fulfill the Lord's will.

Next, Christ sends out his disciples, just as the Father sent him. To be a Christian is to be an envoy of Christ. In Jewish thought the envoy has the same status, carries the same responsibilities and deserves the same respect as the principal who sent the envoy. The responsibility is daunting, to be the representative of Christ who is in turn the representative of the Father. Further, not only am I the envoy of Christ and so of the Father, but also my fellow-Christians; this should make peace between us, and mutual respect.

Then comes the reassuring factor, as he breathes on them his own Spirit. The Christian shares the life-principle of Christ, and lives by his own life. This shows itself, says Paul, not only in the dramatic gifts of the Spirit, the healings, the speaking in tongues, the prophecy and the guidance of the community. It shows itself also in the more humdrum—but still extraordinary—gifts of perseverance, courage, endurance, generosity. Just as no one can say 'Christ is Lord' except through the Spirit, so no one can live these virtues to the extent required of the Christian except by the strength of the Spirit.

### A prayer

*Risen Lord, you breathe on me your Spirit. Help me to take your Spirit to myself and live for you in this strength of your life.*

HW

## John 13:31–32 (NJB)

# *The awe-ful glory*

**Now has the Son of man been glorified, and in him God has been glorified. If God has been glorified in him, God will in turn glorify him in himself, and will glorify him very soon.**

This passage begins the farewell discourse of Jesus after the Last Supper in John's Gospel. It may seem odd that Jesus should be speaking of glorification just before his ultimate humiliation. But for John the passion and resurrection of Jesus forms all one moment, one 'hour'. With typical Johannine double-meaning he speaks of Jesus being 'raised up' on the cross. This means not only his physical lifting onto the high beam of execution but also his exaltation, suggesting his exaltation to the right hand of the Father. Paul writes to the Philippians using the hymn which sings of God giving him the name, 'Lord', which is above every name, as a reward for his humiliation on the cross. For John the two elements make one, single movement of exaltation.

The glory of God is an awesome concept. No human being may see God and live. This is not simply a rule, a commandment laid down. It is a fact of human nature, and its relation to the divine. The godhead bursts the limitations of human nature, so that our limitations simply explode at contact with the divine. If an ant were to understand the human mind, it would need to expand the bounds, or burst the bonds, of its ant-hood. No ant can understand man and live.

The gulf between ant and man is infinitely smaller than that between man and God. Moses' direct experience of God left him with a face calloused and yet shining, so that he had to cover it with a veil. The self-confident prophet Isaiah can only cower and hide before a realization of the majesty of God: 'Go into the rock, hide in the dust, in terror of the Lord, at the brilliance of his majesty, when he arises to make the earth quake'.

At the moment of Jesus' obedience to his Father on the cross the union of God and man becomes complete. Human nature is exploded into God. Jesus does not come back to life, he goes forward into a new life which will be ours.

### A prayer

*Risen Lord, by your suffering and death you went forward into the unspeakable glory of God. Lead me on your path to your same goal.*

HW

Luke 24:28–32 (NJB)

# *The meal that reveals him*

When they drew near to the village to which they were going, he made as if to go on; but they pressed him to stay with them, saying, 'It is nearly evening, and the day is almost over.' So he went in to stay with them. Now while he was with them at table, he took the bread and said the blessing; then he broke it and handed it to them. And their eyes were opened and they recognised him; but he had vanished from their sight. Then they said to each other, 'Did not our hearts burn within us as he talked to us on the road and explained the scriptures to us?'

The story of the two disciples on the road to Emmaus brings the reader from the immediate aftermath of the resurrection to the situation of the Christian today. Without their Lord the two disciples are puzzled and dismayed, out of sorts and purposeless. Life has no meaning. The mysterious stranger explains to them God's plan by means of the scripture, so that their hearts burn within them. It is through the enlightenment of the scripture provided by the risen Lord that they come to have meaning in their lives again, and to recognize the presence in their lives of the Lord. This reaches its climax in their sharing a meal with the Lord, the symbol of lives welded together.

The whole difficulty of attempting to be a Christian is the absence of God, the absence of meaning, the absence of explanation. Yet the Bible reader is such only because of the recognition that attentive listening to the voice of God expressed in the scripture can bring back meaning—and God's meaning—into our lives. The scripture, of course, does not always yield its secret easily; for some time they walked with the stranger without recognizing him.

Nor is the mere listening enough. It is only when the disciples invite the stranger into their lives that the recognition occurs. They must be willing to share with him and to receive from his hands. Perhaps significant also is the reminiscence of the Last Supper: they must be willing to share the commitment to following him in suffering and offering themselves, even to death.

A prayer

*Risen Lord, teach me your way. Give meaning to my life. Come to me with your risen life and share it with me.*

HW

## 1 Corinthians 15:20–21, 42–44 (NJB)

# *First him—then us!*

In fact, however, Christ has been raised from the dead, as the first-fruits of all who have fallen asleep. As it was by one man that death came, so through one man has come the resurrection of the dead. What is sown is perishable, but what is raised is imperishable; what is sown is contemptible, but what is raised is glorious; what is sown is weak, but what is raised is powerful; what is sown is a natural body, and what is raised is a spiritual body.

Christ's resurrection is meaningless unless it has an effect on his followers: he is the first-fruits of all who have fallen asleep, and all who have fallen asleep in Christ are to be transformed as he was. Here Paul is writing to the Christians at Corinth, who were well aware that Christ's Spirit was at work among them. Indeed, it seems that they were too aware, or, more exactly, too aware of the dramatic and extraordinary manifestations of the Spirit.

Paul's reply to their enthusiasm makes two thrusts: firstly, it is not the extraordinary that matters, but rather the way the Spirit can build up the community in love, a love of an intensity and generosity which is impossible without the Spirit of the risen Christ. Secondly, he insists that the transformation in the Spirit is still not complete. There is something still to come, which the living Corinthian community has still not experienced. It is in the resurrection, when people are raised from the dead, that the final change takes place. Then the Christian is brought fully into the sphere of the divine.

That is what each of the changes means. To be perishable and subject to decay is the result of the Fall. To be contemptible and weak is the condition of fallen humanity. But to be imperishable, glorious and powerful is to be suffused with the divinity. The life-principle is no longer to be human nature but the Spirit of God. In such a way is the risen Christ the first-fruits of the new humanity.

### A prayer

*Risen Lord, enter now fully into my life. Amid the contempt, decay and weakness of my present condition bring me to look forward to the future you have in store when you will take me fully to yourself.*

HW

### 1 Corinthians 15:3–6 (NJB)

# 'He was raised to life'

The tradition I handed on to you in the first place, a tradition which I had myself received, was that Christ died for our sins, in accordance with the scriptures, and that he was buried; and that on the third day he was raised to life, in accordance with the scriptures; and that he appeared to Cephas, and later to the Twelve; and next he appeared to more than five hundred of the brothers at the same time, most of whom are still with us, though some have fallen asleep; then he appeared to James and then to all the apostles.

The excitement of this passage of Paul's letter is that one can see the beginning of the tradition of the resurrection. Paul uses the technical terms of the handing on of rabbinic teaching: he 'received' and 'handed on' the tradition. And indeed, there are slight variations from Paul's usual style and vocabulary, which show that he is quoting rather than himself composing freely. This must have been one of the passages which new converts learnt by heart. The only other passage of which we know this is true is the passage on the institution of the eucharist.

So these two were the precious cornerstones of the Christian life and teaching at its very beginning. It was not so much the empty tomb; that was mere negative evidence that Christ did not remain among the dead. Much more important was the appearance of the risen Christ among his followers, the repeated experience of his presence among them and of his new life.

Christianity is a historical religion, but not a religion of the past. It is a living tradition, a continued and continuous experience of the risen life of its Lord among his followers, based on and guaranteed by the appearances to the first disciples.

A prayer

*Risen Lord, you were seen by Peter and his companions. I do not have the privilege of bodily sight of you, but only the blessing of Thomas on those who have not seen but yet have believed. Give me a firm faith and trust in you, that I may always experience you in my life.*

HW

1 Peter 1:3–9 (RSV)

# *Indescribable joy*

Blessed be the God and Father of our Lord Jesus Christ! By his great mercy he has given us a new birth into a living hope through the resurrection of Jesus Christ from the dead, and into an inheritance that is imperishable, undefiled, and unfading, kept in heaven for you, who are being protected by the power of God through faith for a salvation ready to be revealed in the last time. In this you rejoice, even if now for a little while you have had to suffer various trials, so that the genuineness of your faith—being more precious than gold that, though perishable, is tested by fire—may be found to result in praise and glory and honour when Jesus Christ is revealed. Although you have not seen him, you love him; and even though you do not see him now, you believe in him and rejoice with an indescribable and glorious joy, for you are receiving the outcome of your faith, the salvation of your souls.

It is very odd that the Sunday after Easter should be known as Low Sunday. Perhaps people think that this Sunday is less glorious than last Sunday. But that just isn't true.

We are an Easter people, and the glory of 'the resurrection of Jesus Christ from the dead' is with us every day and every hour of our life.

Although in terms of the Church's year we are still waiting for Pentecost and for the pouring out of the Spirit in reality that is always with us. The Spirit has been poured out on us and given to us—and we have 'a living hope'.

No wonder this first letter of Peter shouts for joy—an indescribable and glorious joy—because the writer knows the God and Father of our Lord Jesus Christ who is the cause of all the glory and the blessedness. Easter Sunday wasn't more glorious than today. And those first Christians weren't better off than we are. Every day is one day nearer the last day—when we shall enter into our inheritance. Imperishable, undefiled and unfading Peter says that it is.

Perhaps we could read this passage from Peter over and over again, and think about it and meditate on it, until the glory and the wonder of it streams into our souls.

SB

2 Peter 1:1–4 (NIV)

# *Promises, promises*

Simon Peter, a servant and apostle of Jesus Christ, To those who through the righteousness of our God and Saviour Jesus Christ have received a faith as precious as ours: Grace and peace be yours in abundance through the knowledge of God and of Jesus our Lord. His divine power has given us everything we need for life and godliness through our knowledge of him who called us by his own glory and goodness. Through these he has given us his very great and precious promises.

It is so easy to take the Bible out of context and completely distort its meaning. There is a story of the tractarians preaching on Matthew 18:17—'If he refuses to hear the church, let him be to you as a Gentile'. Apparently they laboured day in, day out, preaching, *ad nauseam* on the text 'hear the church'. The archbishop of the time, Archbishop Whately became so frustrated with their constant ranting on about the church and obeying the ecclesiastical law that he reputedly mounted the pulpit and said, 'My text today is Matthew 18:17, "If he refuses to hear the church, let him!"' We must be so careful to read the whole text, in context, without pretext.

The Bible's promises are often taken out of context. How often have we heard, 'surely I will be with you always'? Yet the promise is set in a context. 'Go and make disciples of all nations... and surely I will be with you always'. Without the 'going' we shall miss the presence of the Lord.

In the opening phrases of his second letter, Peter encourages Christians to claim God's precious promises. He tells us that its through our knowledge of him that we do this.

I often take funerals and I'm struck how many people want Psalm 23. It's very familiar and comforting and I try to help the mourners and friends gain a knowledge of God through reading it. To claim its comfort we need to understand its context. Psalms 22, 23 and 24 go together. Psalm 22 was quoted by Jesus on the cross. Psalm 23 demonstrates God's care, and 24 exalts a glorious future. This promise of God is claimed by kneeling at the cross. Only then can we receive God's shepherd-like love and inherit eternal life.

---

Discover

*Find a promise in the Bible and discover how to experience it.*

GA

### 2 Peter 1:5–9 (NIV)

# *Peter's version of the fruit*

For this very reason, make every effort to add to your faith goodness; and to goodness, knowledge; and to knowledge, self-control; and to self-control, perseverance; and to perseverance, godliness; and to godliness, brotherly kindness; and to brotherly kindness, love. For if you possess these qualities in increasing measure, they will keep you from being ineffective and unproductive in your knowledge of our Lord Jesus Christ. But if anyone does not have them, he is short-sighted and blind.

Peter probably wrote this second letter in the mid to late 60s AD. Paul wrote to the same recipients in Asia Minor in his epistle to the Galatians probably between AD48 and 58. Could it be that Peter copied Paul's fruit of the Spirit in Galatians 5? Maybe he did, maybe he didn't, but there are some striking similarities.

Faith, goodness, knowledge, self control, perseverance, godliness, brotherly kindness and love are Peter's version of the fruit of belonging to Jesus. We are to pick this fruit and add it to our lives for it is in front of us like apples in an orchard.

We used to have a lovely person who helped us clean our house. She was delightful and had very good eyesight but she constantly couldn't see things right in front of her. She used to call me and ask 'Graham, can you see the Mr Sheen?'. 'It's right in front of you', I would say, and point to it on the shelf. After a while I'd get another call 'Graham, where are the bin sacks? Didn't you get any last week?' Again I would point to them at the front of the cupboard. It became quite a joke in the family.

Isn't it easy to miss the obvious? And sometimes it's us who profess to know God most who are the most blind. Our eyes can be so fixed on heaven that we become short-sighted when it comes to the world around us. Like the conservative religious leaders of Jesus' day, the Pharisees, sometimes we remove specks but miss planks.

Peter is about to write about differences between false and true prophets. The ultimate way to discover is to apply the phrase 'by their fruit you shall know them'. It's often the way the world judges us.

### Meditate

*Out of Peter's list of fruit what do I need to work on?*

GD

### 2 Peter 1:16–18 (NIV)

# I—Witness

**We did not follow cleverly invented stories when we told you about the power and coming of our Lord Jesus Christ, but we were eye-witnesses of his majesty. For he received honour and glory from God the Father when the voice came to him from the Majestic Glory, saying, 'This is my Son, whom I love; with him I am well pleased.' We ourselves heard this voice that came from heaven when we were with him on the sacred mountain.**

I often take assemblies in our local school, St Andrew's, as part of a team. This term we have been thinking of saints. We included St Columba and the 'Venomous' Bede, but the other day we tackled the story of St George. What was difficult was to help the children realize that although it's a darn good story, it isn't true in the same way that the story, for example, of St Stephen is true. The legend of St George is, in one sense, not true, yet it contains truth.

Peter refers here to what we now call the Transfiguration—the event on the mountain top when Jesus, Elijah and Moses talked together about what was to come. For Peter this was the ultimate proof that Jesus was the Messiah.

What Peter is keen to impress upon the next generation of believers after Christ is that Jesus is historic. Peter spent time with the him, knew him as a friend and as the glorious Messiah. Jesus was not a cleverly invented legend meant simply to portray truth. He was real.

The more I journey as a Christian, the more I find it important to discover and believe in the historic Jesus. I've found myself wanting to see the land he lived in. Maybe there's a right time for everyone to get in touch with the Bible's history, just as much as there's a time to come to an adult faith, or to put right a particular concern in our lives. When Paul writes in 1 Corinthians 15 that 'Christ died for our sins and was buried', he is reminding us that Jesus was historically real.

I, too, want to become an eye witness in order that I witness more. Perhaps you have been to the Holy Land and it made a difference. I'd be interested to know how that happened.

### Question

*What difference does it make to know Jesus really did live?*

GD

## 2 Peter 1:19–21 (NIV)

# True prophets

And we have the word of the prophets made more certain, and you will do well to pay attention to it, as to a light shining in a dark place, until the day dawns and the morning star rises in your hearts. Above all, you must understand that no prophecy of Scripture came about by the prophet's own interpretation. For prophecy never had its origin in the will of man, but men spoke from God as they were carried along by the Holy Spirit.

'Thus sayeth the Lord', the oldish man said in the prayer meeting. 'You will not die, but I will take you unto me like I did my servant Isaiah'. There was a long confused silence. Then the same voice began again. 'Thus sayeth the Lord, I'm sorry I made a mistake it was Elijah wasn't it.' Some prophecies just have that smack of being human!

Yet at other times in church I've heard tiny hesitant voices saying the most profound things, usually very unadorned with religious language and often offered rather than imposed.

A few years ago Bishop Jim Thompson asked me to be a part of our diocesan conference planning group. As we struggled with the theme and speakers for the conference we thought of all the Bishops and theologians that we knew. Which should we have? When Bishop Jim heard what we were planning he asked us to consider people from secular life. It seemed strange to begin with and many clergy in the diocese objected. 'How shall we hear God with these people coming to speak?', they asked. There were some who categorically refused to come. However when it happened it was the best conference I've ever been to. The speakers didn't profess to be church-goers but they spoke prophetically.

For me there are two types of prophecy. One which I trust implicitly, the inspired word of God in the Bible, another which I hear in everyday life and need to test. Both types reveal something of the nature of God and his purpose for creation. Both speak into today's society and our lives in particular. Both come not by human will but by divine inspiration, and like Peter I can say that when I see either I am attracted to the message like a light in a dark place.

### Consider

*What have I heard recently which I would describe as prophecy? What shall I do about it?*

GD

## 2 Peter 2:1–3 (NIV)

# *False prophets*

But there were also false prophets among the people, just as there will be false teachers among you. They will secretly introduce destructive heresies, even denying the sovereign Lord who bought them—bringing swift destruction on themselves. Many will follow their shameful ways and will bring the way of truth into disrepute. In their greed these teachers will exploit you with stories they have made up. Their condemnation has long been hanging over them, and their destruction has not been sleeping.

In the first section of his letter, Peter, the perennial pastor, endeavours to stimulate growth in the Christians to whom he writes. Now in the middle section he seeks to warn of false prophecy leading to heresy. It's a lesson for all times

I was preaching recently on Samson. One thing that stood out was the way in which the Philistines managed to knock Israel off course with God. They didn't invade the land so much as infiltrate it. Rather than an all-out attack which can be obviously seen and resisted they employed a more subtle means of leading the people of God astray. Intermarriage—against God's commands—and false teaching in the ordinary ways of life (food, recreation) slowly made Israel turn from its Lord.

I suspect that false teaching always takes this form. Where we expect to find it is in the huge doctrines of the church, amongst the creeds or the articles of our faith. Where it really dwells is in the everyday things of life, such as how we spend our money, how we teach our children, and how we conduct our relationships.

The result of false teaching is a denial of the sovereign Lord, and the result of that is a 'swift destruction'. But Peter turns the sense of the passage. Ironically what the false prophet tries to achieve backfires on him or her. After the words 'swift destruction' he adds 'on themselves'.

Reading a book on management by John Harvey Jones the other day I noted his principle of 'judo'. The aim is to turn the strength of your opponent against himself, so defeating him in the process. Although false prophets seek to destroy the church, what in fact they achieve is their own destruction.

### Prayer

*From all evil and mischief;*
*from pride, vanity, and hypocrisy;*
*from envy, hatred, and malice;*
*and from all evil intent,*
*Good Lord, deliver us.*

from the Litany, ASB

GD

2 Peter 2:5–9 (NIV)

# *Postmodernism*

If he [God] did not spare the ancient world when he brought the flood on its ungodly people, but protected Noah, a preacher of righteousness, and seven others; if he condemned the cities of Sodom and Gomorrah by burning them to ashes, and made them an example of what is going to happen to the ungodly; and if he rescued Lot, a righteous man, who was distressed by the filthy lives of lawless men... then the Lord knows how to rescue godly men from trials and to hold the unrighteous for the day of judgment, while continuing their punishment.

There are many unpopular words around at the moment. I remember one person walking out of a school assembly I once took because I'd mentioned the word 'sin'. Yet by throwing out words like Hell, punishment, repentance and sin we may find we've thrown out heaven, reward, joy and redemption too. Peter gives some reasons here why we need to consider these things.

Firstly, God knows the difference between good and evil. Whereas our postmodern world has confused and smudged the edges of morality so much that the whole picture seems like water-colours in the rain, God sees clearly. If we are to as well, we need to train ourselves. There are things the Bible tells us to do, and things it tells us not to do. When we begin to examine those things, then we begin to recognize good from evil.

God has shown in history how he deals with people. He is merciful. 'But thou art the same Lord whose proper-ty is always to have mercy', the Prayer Book says. At the root of the concept of mercy lies forgiveness. It's not about excusing. Its about reaching up in sorrow to be gripped by the hand that will pull us out of the mire.

But God is also just. Stewart Henderson's poem about justice being 'just ice' sums up the view many have. Their perception of God's justice leaves them cold and somewhat confused. Yet justice does not need to be like this. Justice offers the victim of the bully a warmth and security previously unknown.

Peter has discovered the principle that God is moral, merciful and just. It is in the trinity of these attributes that some find their rescue, and others their destruction.

---

## Meditate

*In what ways does my life show this trinity too?*

GD

### Luke 24:28–32 (NIV)

# *Abide with me...*

As they approached the village to which they were going, Jesus acted as if he were going further. But they urged him strongly, 'Stay with us for it is nearly evening; the day is almost over.' So he went in to stay with them. When he was at the table with them he took bread, gave thanks, broke it and began to give it to them. Then their eyes were opened and they recognised him, and he disappeared from their sight. They asked each other, 'Were not our hearts burning within us while he talked with us on the road and opened the Scriptures to us?'

Lord as I walk with you, you teach me. It's not the kind of lesson I had at school but it's a living discovery of the profound in the simple. The other day I went to a museum of science and saw a well made from mirrors and as I looked in it the images went on for ever. You're like that, a deep well of light.

Lord as you're about to go on, I too want to ask you to stay. It's not that I want you all to myself it's just I don't want to be without you. If you went on and I stayed here, I know it wouldn't work. It would soon become tedious and unchallenging and staid and stale. I want you to stay because I want my family to meet you and for you to share in the home we enjoy.

Lord you take the simplest of things and make them so real; the taking of bread, breaking of bread, giving thanks, and sharing it. Your patterns are so easy to understand and so exciting. They speak to my heart and satisfy my mind. They excite me and move me and make me want to find out more.

Lord I love that feeling of my heart burning with you. It's that moment of recognition, like when Mary said to you 'Rabboni' in the garden after you called her by name; like here when the disciples suddenly *knew* it was you. What a moment, like coming home.

#### Reflect

*Like calm in place of clamour,*
  *like peace that follows pain,*
*Like meeting after parting,*
  *like sunshine after rain;*
*Like moonlight and starlight*
  *and sunlight on the sea,*
*so is my Lord, my living Lord,*
  *so is my Lord to me.*

Timothy Dudley-Smith

*GD*

2 Peter 2:10–12 (NIV)

# *Born to be caught*

This is especially true of those who follow the corrupt desire of the sinful nature and despise authority. Bold and arrogant, these men are not afraid to slander celestial beings; yet even angels, although they are stronger and more powerful, do not bring slanderous accusations against such beings in the presence of the Lord. But these men blaspheme in matters they do not understand. They are like brute beasts, creatures of instinct, born only to be caught and destroyed, and like beasts they too will perish.

I love taking weddings rehearsals. The bride and groom arrive at the church and I go through the service with them. I've noticed that more and more people tend to come to the rehearsal. Some ten years ago it was often just the couple but now the bridesmaids come along as well as the parents and the page-boys, the photographer, the video operator, the flower arranger. Once even the chauffeur turned up! It's like being a shepherd herding all these people into the pews. I disappear off into the vestry to talk over the service the couple want. There are two possible services, one from the old Prayer Book and the other from the new ASB (well, 1980!).

Quite often the couple begin by wanting the old service with its beautiful poetic language. The text goes like this: '[Marriage] is not by any to be enterprized, nor taken in hand unadvisedly, lightly, or wantonly, to satisfy men's carnal lusts and appetites, like brute beasts that have no understanding'. How the couple's faces drop. 'You can't say that, I'm not a brute beast,' retorts the man and the service is quickly changed.

Far be it from me to accuse anyone of being a brute beast, yet humankind 'en masse' does tend to show itself up at times. Atrocities never cease to amaze me in their intensity. I heard the other day of a handicapped lad being beaten by his father because he was lazy!

Peter speaks here of those who are spiritual and carnal thugs. He condemns them as those who are born to be caught. It is difficult to eradicate these brutal acts which emanate from the beast within. Maybe we have to start with our own inner lives for we all have the capacity to injure others, and most likely the ones we love most.

Imagine

*What sort of creature is a brute beast? How can it be dealt with? In what ways does it raise its head in my life?*
GD

### 2 Peter 2:17–19 (NIV)

# A dry oasis

These men are springs without water and mists driven by a storm. Blackest darkness is reserved for them. For they mouth empty, boastful words and, by appealing to the lustful desires of sinful human nature, they entice people who are just escaping from those who live in error. They promise them freedom, while they themselves are slaves of depravity—for a man is a slave to whatever has mastered him.

My father used to say to me 'you don't go into the ministry for the money', but quite some time ago we found we had the opportunity to buy a new car, a brand new one. We were excited about it and chose a silver one. The advertising told us we couldn't dream of anything better and that all our cares and worries would disappear if we bought one of these types of cars. We even chose the number-plate and the day came to drive it home. It purred out of the garage but that was about the last time it did. I must have gone back to the garage twice every month with that car. The 'timing' kept going wrong, it ran on after the engine was stopped, it 'hunted' at every junction. It was a real disappointment and all the garage could say was that they'd fixed it every time we took it back. The promise of a carefree life was completely untrue.

False prophets are springs without water, mists driven by a storm. Peter is saying that there is no substance at the end of their promises. A dry oasis is no oasis at all. The promise of rain from an approaching mist disappears before dropping its much needed water. Like the advertising for my car, there's lots of hype but no reality.

In fact much of the advertising I see today is based, often subtly, on false promises. 'Buy this and you get all this as well'. In many parts of our world we see and hear promises which end up in disappointment, if not despair. The multinationals who deliberately create dependencies in Third World countries, then rocket the price or withdraw altogether are also promising heaven and delivering hell.

### Think

*What a difference it would make if all Christians took a stand to eradicate one false promise from our neighbourhoods.*

GL

## 2 Peter 2:20–22 (NIV)

# Better not to have known

If they have escaped the corruption of the world by knowing our Lord and Saviour Jesus Christ and are again entangled in it and overcome, they are worse off at the end than they were at the beginning. It would have been better for them not to have known the way of righteousness, than to have known it and then to turn their backs on the sacred command that was passed on to them. Of them the proverbs are true: 'A dog returns to its vomit,' and, 'A sow that is washed goes back to her wallowing in the mud.'

Peter does use some choice imagery here, pretty crude but striking. Knowing God and tasting what his friendship is like is wonderful. Returning to the world's menu again is as bad as the disgusting things dogs and other animals do. I remember Amber, our golden retriever, being sick once. In the time that it took me to get a bowl, fill it with water and put on the rubber gloves, she'd wolfed the lot. Ugh! It's disgusting to think of it. Occasionally she might get up on the bed, or give one of the children a big lick on the face, but she is after all a dog and can be pretty grotesque. Peter uses a shocking image to compare a life with God to a life back in the world.

The big question in this passage is whether, having become a Christian, it is possible to lose salvation. My studies, particularly in Hebrews, suggest to me that it is. It can't happen by chance, but I do believe we retain responsibility to go on believing. In fact to be spiritually fresh it is important to be aware of this responsibility.

In an ideal world children would be brought up by Christian parents who provided teaching and an example of how to live the Christian life. In due course they would come to an adult faith for themselves. Sadly that is obviously not the case. Many children of Christian parents, indeed most, fall away from faith through ignorance or apathy. Can this be the case with adult Christians too? If we do not go on taking spiritual food can we expect to live? Shall we lose our salvation through neglect or our own deliberate fault? I wouldn't want to fall out with anyone over this, I may in the end be wrong but it certainly seems a possibility.

### Think

*What parts of my own salvation am I responsible for?*

GD

### 2 Peter 3:8–10 (NIV)

# Don't forget this

But do not forget this one thing, dear friends: With the Lord a day is like a thousand years, and a thousand years are like a day. The Lord is not slow in keeping his promise, as some understand slowness. He is patient with you, not wanting anyone to perish, but everyone to come to repentance. But the day of the Lord will come like a thief. The heavens will disappear with a roar; the elements will be destroyed by fire, and the earth and everything in it will be laid bare.

Chapter 3 of Peter's letter changes its emphasis and becomes an encouragement to watch for the end times. As we approach 2000, we too hear and see many theories of the end times.

We may be wondering if Jesus will ever return as he said. It does seem a long time since his first coming.

The problem that faced the not so early Christians, the first generation after Christ, was that he was expected to come back almost immediately but there was no sign of him. So Peter writes that God has not forgotten them, but a thousand years can be like a day to him.

I read a book some time ago that took this literally. The author mapped out a possible time for Christ's return based on the literal years from Adam and Eve to the present day. Back to Christ was two thousand years or two days, back to Abraham before Christ was another two thousand, and tracing the literal years in the generations before Abraham, he managed to get another two thousand. Six days in all seemed to him to suggest that at the turn of this millennium Christ would return.

A number of people thought about it in Walcot and we had a debate on it. Although I couldn't accept much of what the author said, three things struck me. First, we are not speaking very much into the significance of the millennium. Two thousand years from what? It is a good opportunity to tell of what Christian life is all about.

Secondly, there is great enthusiasm when we begin to think of these things. Heaven is exciting!

Thirdly, in our consumer world we tend to think that when the end comes the world will be dispensed with, thrown away. But God's purpose is to renew. Perhaps we need to think more carefully of how God will renew amongst such destruction.

### Question

*What do you think prevents Jesus from returning?*

GD

## 2 Peter 3:11–13 (NIV)

# *Looking forward*

Since everything will be destroyed in this way, what kind of people ought you to be? You ought to live holy and godly lives as you look forward to the day of God and speed its coming. That day will bring about the destruction of the heavens by fire, and the elements will melt in the heat. But in keeping with his promise we are looking forward to a new heaven and a new earth, the home of righteousness.

The promise that Peter is referring to is in Isaiah 65. 'Behold I will create new heavens and a new earth' It's repeated in Revelation 21 which is often read at funerals. It speaks of a time when there will be no more tears or pain or death. I remember a year ago when a parishioner died in Walcot. Gill was not old and was very much loved in the church. She left several children and a wonderful husband. She really was, like Peter describes here, holy and godly.

She planned her funeral and we carried it out according to her wishes. At one point we did a rather brave thing. We asked the congregation if anyone wanted to say anything about Gill. After one or two comments the churchwarden's wife came to the front. She spoke simply and plainly without affect about a picture of Gill. Jesus was on a hill and Gill came running into his arms with great joy and delight.

This vision was so powerful in such a quiet way it really did seem prophetic. I had seen Gill just before she died in hospital, weak with the cancer, finding it hard to breathe and not even able to sit up, never mind run anywhere. But Gill had been renewed in the picture, her new life involved a new body and the most wonderful love. The two pictures have stayed with me and become part of my grieving. It feels sometimes this is what we are called to carry. The picture reflecting the 'as it is' and another about how it will be. They combine to give us reality and hope. At the end of the day Christ shows us not only how to live, but also how to die.

### Pray

*Reveal thyself before my closing eyes;*
*Shine through the gloom, and point*
*me to the skies,*
*Heaven's morning breaks, and earth's*
*vain shadows flee;*
*In life, in death, O Lord, abide with me.*

Henry Francis Lyte

GD

### 2 Peter 3:14–16 (NIV)

# *Patience means salvation*

So then, dear friends, since you are looking forward to this, make every effort to be found spotless, blameless and at peace with him. Bear in mind that our Lord's patience means salvation, just as our dear brother Paul also wrote to you with the wisdom that God gave him. He writes the same way in all his letters, speaking in them of these matters. His letters contain some things that are hard to understand, which ignorant and unstable people distort, as they do the other Scriptures, to their own destruction.

The cradle of Christian leadership is a well-balanced team working together for the kingdom. Much is made of the conflict between Peter and Paul: how Paul had to correct Peter's thinking about circumcision and so on. It's rare to hear how the two got on together but throughout this letter it is clear that Peter holds Paul in great esteem.

A cradle is supported at either end by rockers which gently sway the cradle to bring peace. Similarly in the early Christian church Peter and Paul stand as examples of holy rocks who together preach the peace of Christ. The 'dear friends' were looking forward to the time when a new heaven and new earth was coming, a home of righteousness. Peter and Paul, by their teaching and caring and examples, offer a cradle of two attributes which are crucial to the Christian life, namely patience and peace.

When I left theological college the wife of a lecturer, Jeanne Wesson, gave me an egg-timer to remind me that I must pace myself in my ministry. She was prophetic in her gift to me. Patience can build peace, and the lack of it can wreck peace both individually and as a church. Peter had learnt this directly from Jesus. After all he was the one who was always rushing and risking. Who leapt from the boat to walk on the water? Who impetuously told Jesus he would never deny him? Who cut off the ear of Malchus when Jesus was arrested? Peter needed an egg-timer as well. There are always some people in churches who rush around like Peter. I find that they irritate others, but we need to remember that Jesus never excluded Peter. He rebuked him and penetrated his impetuosity but he never abandoned him.

### Think

*Who reminds me of Peter in my church and friends? How can I love them as Jesus loved Peter?*

GD

## Isaiah 61:1–3 (GNB)

# *Christed people: a reflection*

When Jesus stood up in the synagogue at the start of his ministry he took the scroll of Isaiah and started to read from it. The prophetic words described the ministry of the Christ, the anointed one. He fulfilled them perfectly—and then after his death and resurrection poured out his Spirit on us. So now we are anointed people, the 'christed' ones. Now we can reflect on God's purpose for us, and his promises to us, in those same words that Jesus used at the start of his ministry.

Now we can say 'The Sovereign Lord has filled me with his spirit'—because to be a Christian is to have the Spirit of Christ living within us. And he will continue to anoint and fill us, day after day, as we pray.

Now we can say 'He has chosen me and sent me:

'To bring good news to the poor'— the good news of the love of God and the forgiveness of sins. Because I know it myself I can offer it to other people.

'To heal the broken-hearted'. If my own heart has been broken, for whatever reason—because of my own sin, or because of someone else's, or because someone has hurt and rejected me—and if I know something of the healing of Christ, then I have something to say to other people whose hearts have been broken.

'To announce release to captives and freedom to those in prison'. If I know something of the freedom from sin which Christ gives to us, then I can tell other people about the release that he offers us. Like the release which Charles Wesley wrote about : 'Long my imprisoned spirit lay, Fast bound in sin and nature's night; Thine eye diffused a quickening ray, I woke, the dungeon flamed with light; My chains fell off, my heart was free; I rose, went forth, and followed Thee.

Now we can say:

He has sent me to proclaim that the time has come when the Lord will save his people and defend their enemies. He has sent me to comfort all who mourn, to give to those who mourn in Zion joy and gladness instead of grief, a song of praise instead of sorrow.

If we know something of what it is to have our sorrow transmuted into joy, and our sad songs turned into songs of praise, then we have got something to sing about and something to tell other people.

They will be like trees that the Lord himself has planted. They will all do what is right, and God will be praised for what he has done.

*SB*

## Psalm 23 (RSV)

# *God guides and God provides*

The Lord is my shepherd, I shall not want; he makes me lie down in green pastures. He leads me beside still waters; he restores my soul. He leads me in paths of righteousness for his name's sake. Even though I walk through the valley of the shadow of death, I fear no evil; for thou art with me; thy rod and thy staff, they comfort me. Thou preparest a table before me in the presence of my enemies; thou anointest my head with oil, my cup overflows. Surely goodness and mercy shall follow me all the days of my life; and I shall dwell in the house of the Lord for ever.

The background of Psalm 23 is a dry ground where pasture for the sheep is not obvious but has to be sought. To save the sheep from exhaustion there has to be a midday rest, at best in some place where a stream is at hand. The shepherd knows every inch of the landscape and leads his flock to the most beneficial places. Owing to the nature of the territory the very life of the sheep depends on the care and knowledge of the shepherd. They could not exist without him.

The Psalm spells out the conviction that God will care for his people, which meant not only the nation of Israel but individuals like you and me, now, in our very different world. He is the same God. And he will not only lead us and defend us. He will provide for us: whatever our circumstances, he knows our needs. And there will be no end to his goodness. 'Surely goodness and mercy shall follow me all the days of my life.' Can we rest in this? Can we let it take away fear of the future—the sort of worry that can keep us awake at night? How shall I manage if my sight becomes worse than it is? How much longer can I keep this house and home going? Make Psalm 23 your own and notice how many times the word 'me' occurs in it. It deals with individual fears of people like you and me: the young, the middle aged and the old.

### Prayer

*Praise be to thee, O Lord, for leading me and providing for me thus far.*
*Inspire me to trust you implicitly for the rest of life's journey right up to its glorious end.*

*DCF*

### Psalm 24:1–5, 7 (RSV)

# *Entering into God's presence*

The earth is the Lord's and the fullness thereof, the world and those who dwell therein; for he has founded it upon the seas, and established it upon the rivers. Who shall ascend the hill of the Lord? And who shall stand in his holy place? He who has clean hands and a pure heart, who does not lift up his soul to what is false, and does not swear deceitfully. He will receive blessing from the Lord, and vindication from the God of his salvation... Lift up your heads, O gates! and be lifted up, O ancient doors! that the King of glory may come in.

If you are reading this in the train, or at home keeping one eye on the baby, you won't readily see what relevance a piece of Hebrew history 3,000 years old can have to you. Indeed I wouldn't touch upon it did I not know that it can light up the words of this Psalm and give them meaning for us today. So let me sketch in the background. King David had been driven from pillar to post before being established in his kingdom with its capital on Mount Zion. But at long last he beat his enemies down and made Mount Zion his own. There he would establish the temple of the Lord, for the Lord had given him the victory. And the day would come, and that soon, when with a great triumphal procession representatives of the nation would ceremonially enter the city knocking on its gates. What a day! But who would make up the triumphal procession? Anybody? Blasphemers? Liars? Cruel people? Traitors? Burglars? Rapists?

Yes, they were all mixed up in the nation as they are today. But only the people who had not lifted up their souls to what was corrupt and false would be able actually to pass through the gates and enter the city.

And that is how it is for us. We can only come into the real presence of God if our hands and heart are clean when we kneel down in prayer, or worship in church, or seek a message from the Lord. That is why we begin by asking for God's forgiveness.

### Prayer

*Lord, I come into your presence now just where I am and as I am; I know you will receive me for my confidence is in your grace and not in my worthiness.*

DCF

## Psalm 25:9–13 (RSV)

# *Check your rebellion*

He leads the humble in what is right, and teaches the humble his way. All the paths of the Lord are steadfast love and faithfulness, for those who keep his covenant and his testimonies. For thy name's sake, O Lord, pardon my guilt, for it is great. Who is the man that fears the Lord? Him will he instruct in the way that he should choose. He himself shall abide in prosperity, and his children shall posses the land.

Today I am feeling rebellious. I know I shouldn't be but I am, and I know I must come out of the mood. This is why I must take this Psalm 25 to myself. The fact is I am here in a convalescent home taking rather a long time to recover from back trouble. I long to be returning home and looking after myself, but I can't at present. No, I am not asking for sympathy, many people are in a far worse condition than I; and the people looking after me are very kind. They are not Anglican, but genuine Christians, and the opportunity to be here came out of the blue. I shall find my strength again, but not if I rebel. I must accept that God knows all about this and has some purpose in it.

I have to keep Philippians 4:11 in mind: 'I know how to be abased, and I know how to abound... I can do all things in him who strengthens me.' But first of all we have to be meek. A rebellious attitude will accomplish nothing. We cannot fight ourselves into what we want, even our state of health. We have to accept what God allows. And we have to believe that he will teach us his way, yes, the way he chooses for us.

Forgive me for letting myself intrude into today's reading and comment, but the Psalms did grow out of personal, human experience, some riotously happy, some limiting and hard to bear. Unless we are willing to enter into this, including the rough patches, what the Psalmist has to say to us will be little more than empty words.

What I have had to learn these last weeks is how to be cheerfully dependent on other people. It is easy to fall into the trap of self-sufficiency when strong and well, especially if you are a leader in the community, and we need leaders. But this is not the whole story. Even leaders need to remember their dependence on God and his will for them. This is what it means for the leader to be meek.

### Prayer

*Lord, forgive me my rebellious spirit. I want to go the way you choose for me.*

DCF

## Psalm 26:1–4, 8, 12 (RSV)

# *Christian lifestyle*

Vindicate me, O Lord, for I have walked in my integrity, and I have trusted in the Lord without wavering. Prove me, O Lord, and try me; test my heart and my mind. For thy steadfast love is before my eyes, and I walk in faithfulness to thee. I do not sit with false men, nor do I consort with dissemblers;... O Lord, I love the habitation of thy house, and the place where thy glory dwells... My foot stands on level ground; in the great congregation I will bless the Lord.

What is your lifestyle? What is my lifestyle? I mean as a Christian. You may be an engineer, a schoolteacher, a nurse, an architect, a musician, a housewife, or have some other calling. I am not asking about your lifestyle as any one of these, nor even of your lifestyle independent of your specific calling whatever it may be. I am asking about your lifestyle *as a Christian*, my lifestyle as a Christian. Let there be no misunderstanding: the Christian believer should live differently from the unbeliever. How? Well, read Psalm 26 again and it will tell you. A Christian must be known for personal integrity, for consistency and reliability because of trust in God. He or she must live in the consciousness of God's love and care for individuals and keep away from empty triflers, people who are never serious, people who are always fooling about, always with an eye for taking passing pleasures. This does not mean Christians must always be solemn men and women with no lightness in their characters, heavy-handed individuals. God forbid! But essentially different, different from the silly, the lightweights and the ne'er-do-wells. Christians must be distinctive in their way of going about life, they must stand out. In a way, they must shine.

There is one other verse to note in our reading today—verse 8. 'I have loved the habitation of thy house and the place where thy honour dwelleth.' It may not always be easy to testify to our faith by word of mouth or even to be opportune and wise. Here, however, is a place to begin. Let yourself be *seen* as a consistent church goer. This never fails to convey the existence of one's faith.

### Prayer

*Lord, make me a consistent Christian, a man, a woman seen to be different; but humble, not proud and not sanctimonious, knowing that all I have is of your goodness.*

DCF

## Psalm 27:1–6 (RSV)

# *On top*

The Lord is my light and my salvation; whom shall I fear? The Lord is the stronghold of my life; of whom shall I be afraid? When evildoers assail me, uttering slanders against me, my adversaries and foes, they shall stumble and fall. Though a host encamp against me, my heart shall not fear; though war arise against me, yet I will be confident. One thing have I asked of the Lord, that will I seek after; that I may dwell in the house of the Lord all the days of my life, to behold the beauty of the Lord, and to inquire in his temple. For he will hide me in his shelter in the day of trouble; he will conceal me under the cover of his tent, he will set me high upon a rock. And now my head shall be lifted up above my enemies round about me; and I will offer in his tent sacrifices with shouts of joy; I will sing and make melody to the Lord.

We can't always be 'on top'. Things go wrong sometimes, people disappoint us, jobs fail, we may even be thrown out of work. The sun does not perpetually shine in clear skies, storms can blow up flattening our crops, a car can break down just when we need it. Life is a thing of ups and downs. Today's Psalm tells us how not to be permanently down, perhaps with a scowling face and sharp, angry eyes, the kind of person we instinctively avoid. The way is to keep in mind verse 1 of this Psalm, 'The Lord is my light and my salvation; whom then shall I fear, the Lord is the stronghold of my life, of whom shall I be afraid?' Say the words out loud.

This is an area of life where the example of other Christians can help us. When we see how they have 'coped', as we say, working their way steadily through hardships and handicaps with a ready smile not far away from their faces and a helping hand quick to be extended, we see what we should be and what we should do. So make sure you read Christian biographies and keep company with people who have made an impact by their steadfastness and cheerfulness under trial.

### Prayer

*Lord, lift me up above the commonplace,*
*above the dismally defeated,*
*above the perpetually gloomy.*
*Let me be a light among my associates.*
*Make Psalm 27 real to me.*

DCF

### Psalm 28:1–3, 6, 7 (RSV)

# *A song on my lips*

To thee, O Lord, I call; my rock, be not deaf to me, lest, if thou be silent to me, I become like those who go down to the Pit. Hear the voice of my supplication, as I cry to thee for help, as I lift up my hands toward thy most holy sanctuary. Take me not off with the wicked, with those who are workers of evil, who speak peace with their neighbours, while mischief is in their hearts... Blessed be the Lord! for he has heard the voice of my supplications. The Lord is my strength and my shield; in him my heart trusts; so I am helped, and my heart exults, and with my song I give thanks to him.

Psalm 28 is a prayer. It is also about prayer, prayer when everything seems to be up against us. Actually everything may not be 'up against us', but so it seems. We feel desperate. We do not know which way to turn. And if God is silent, or seems to be silent, we shall be people without a future. So please God, hear our prayer, let us not go down with the godless.

The Psalmist 'came through'. God heard his supplication so that he cried out, 'The Lord is my strength and my shield'. It was a gasp of relief and a heartfelt conviction. In consequence he was a new man, a man with a working faith. And it all grew out of bitter experience, the hurting experience of going down and rising up in sheer desperation. Would he ever forget? 'My heart trusts, so I am helped.' And now he was scarcely recognizable. 'My heart exalts', he said (present tense note). His joy was ongoing. He certainly sang and his song was one of praise.

There is something wrong with our Christian life if our hearts do not greatly rejoice and if there is no song on our lips. Religious devotion is unwholesome if it lacks constant praise. It may be that we have never gone down to the depths in life, it may be that we do not know what it feels like to resurface again. More likely is that we do not appreciate how God has delivered us, changing our whole life and demeanour in answer to our prayer.

---

### Prayer

*Lord, you have brought me
through troubles in my life,
some big troubles,
some little troubles.
Today I bow my head
in thanksgiving and praise.
You have been my helper.
Praise be to you, O Lord,
our caring God.*

DCF

### John 6:9 (RSV)

# God will use the little you give

**There is a lad here who has five barley loaves and two fish, but what are they among so many?**

Here is a boy wondering what to do on a fine almost summer's day. So his mother said, 'Here is a picnic, go out for today.' So she wrapped up five bread rolls, added two fish, gave them to him and sent him off. Boy-like, he wondered aimlessly along, his picnic in his pocket.

Then he saw a crowd listening to a preacher in the open air. They were captivated by him and the boy couldn't help listening too. He liked the look of the preacher. When the preacher appeared to want to feed the hungry crowds, because it was growing late, he appealed to the men standing by to feed them. But they, like the people, were destitute of food. Then the boy remembered his picnic and took it out of his pocket. One of the men, seeing this, said to the preacher, 'There is a lad here who has five barley loaves and two fish, but what are they among so many.' Nevertheless they asked him for his picnic and because he liked the look of the preacher he gave it up. And somehow, he didn't know how, all those hundreds and hundreds of people were fed from his tiny packet. In short, the boy gave his little and the crowds were fed.

You tell me, you are a very ordinary Christian. You lack the gifts to speak at big meetings, you cannot organize the church finances, you can't offer for work in the mission field, you have a family to care for. What can you offer in the way of Christian service? Yes, you try to keep up your churchgoing, the neighbours see you making your way to church on Sundays. O but it is so little, so tiny in comparison with the great task of the Christian mission.

But don't forget the boy. He gave his little and Christ made it much. It astonished him. And one day you will be astonished at what your little piece of Christian witness has accomplished. It is true the crowd would not have been fed without Christ's miraculous power, but neither would they without the boy. Don't forget the boy. He could be you.

### Prayer

*Take the little I have to offer this Sunday,*
*and use it for the welfare of others*
*in ways only you, O Lord, know how.*
DCF

Psalm 29:1–6, 10–11 (RSV)

# Hear and speak the word

Ascribe to the Lord, O heavenly beings, ascribe to the Lord glory and strength. Ascribe to the Lord the glory of his name; worship the Lord in holy array. The voice of the Lord is upon the waters; the God of glory thunders, the Lord, upon many waters. The voice of the Lord is powerful, the voice of the Lord is full of majesty. The voice of the Lord breaks the cedars, the Lord breaks the cedars of Lebanon. He makes Lebanon to skip like a calf, and Sirion like a young wild ox... The Lord sits enthroned over the flood; the Lord sits enthroned as king for ever. May the Lord give strength to his people! May the Lord bless his people with peace!

This Psalm is about the word of God, here called 'God's voice'. It tells us with a variety of figures of speech that it is powerful. God's word does things. It breaks, it thunders, it spits fire— verse 7: 'the voice of the Lord flashes forth flames of fire'; but it also brings forth new life and activity. God's voice is full of majesty and power. And so is God's word. This is the message for us from this Psalm.

The Church is called to minister God's word. It is conveyed to us through the pages of the Bible. There is, of course, the ministry of healing, and the exercise of compassion for all in need, but with it there must come the word of God for it is precisely there that the power lies. And in worship the word of God must be proclaimed. It must be spoken and heard. This is accomplished through intelligent reading of the Scriptures and with the expectancy that it will produce results. Do those who read the lessons in church really expect them to accomplish anything? And there is preaching. A church without preaching is never an effective church. And the preaching calls for skill with language and presentation. Then the word becomes embodied in the preacher, it is enfleshed, it can be seen in the preacher's eyes, his hands, the movement of his head, indeed his body language; and behind it all is the preacher's commitment of body and soul in his personal devotion to Christ our Lord who is the *Word of God*.

## Psalm 30:5 (RSV)

# For the Christian unhappiness does not last

**For his anger is but for a moment and his favour is for a lifetime. Weeping may tarry for the night, but joy comes with the morning.**

Occasionally we should recall our rough periods in the past. Was it an illness we thought would never recur? Was it a ghastly wartime experience? Was it a financial crash making our future look frighteningly bleak? Was it that time of exile in a foreign land? Was it, is it, that horrible emptiness after bereavement? They were hurting times and we wish to forget them. But don't forget them. And for this reason, they tell us that the bad times did not last forever, they passed away, though no doubt leaving scars.

Life isn't all rough, not all the way, not all the time. Ultimately the sun breaks through, the stars shine and the birds sing. We should never submit to dreariness, never reckon that everything goes wrong for me. This is not so. Life is a series of variations. To change the metaphor, 'We need to take the rough with the smooth.' Yes, there will be rough patches, but there will also be smooth patches. So don't live 'down in the dumps'. Some people unfortunately do grub along down there, and they are not a pleasure to meet.

Remember this is God's world. He has made life a thing of ups and downs. We shall experience roughness but not perpetual roughness. 'Weeping may endure for the night, but joy comes with the morning.' I am writing this at a time of painful back trouble necessitating some weeks in hospital. Shall I ever get strong again? Are you surprised if I hang on to Psalm 30 verse 5?

Yes, at times God lets us be hurt. Because he knows that he will bring us out again into the sunlight, not perhaps in the way we expect but certainly and truly. And this is how we have to learn and trust God and to wait upon him. In our times of prosperity, health and happiness we may boast 'I shall never be moved' (Psalm 30:6). We reckon our health and safety is in our capable hands, but this is not so. Is this why we have at times to be brought low? Verses 11 and 12 of this Psalm say: 'Thou hast turned for me my mourning into dancing... that my soul may praise thee and not be silent.'

Prayer

*Open my eyes, O Lord
to see the rough places of life aright.*
*DCF*

Psalm 31:14-16 (RSV)

# *God guides his servants*

But I trust in thee, O Lord,
I say, 'Thou art my God.'
My times are in thy hand;
    deliver me from the hand of my
    enemies and persecutors!
Let thy face shine on thy servant;
    save me in thy steadfast love!

The verse that grips me here is, 'My times are in thy hand'. I have believed this for many a long year and still believe it. God prepares the way for those who trust him.

Let me tell you a story. More than fifty years ago a vicar informed his congregation that a mission was to take place in the town; some students would take part. He appealed for offers to put them up.

Hearing of this a young woman told him of a couple who would help in this way but asked that a man, not a young student, be sent, but someone with ability to make out a case for the Christian gospel because the husband, a businessman, was showing interest.

I found myself billeted in that very comfortable home knowing nothing of all this.

About three days after my settling in, my hostess announced that she would like me to meet a very elegant young woman who had helped them in the Christian faith. Next day she ushered her into the drawing room.

I was captivated. I admit it. And when on the sofa she asked me an intelligent question about a verse in the prologue to St John's Gospel, I was captivated even more.

Not surprisingly, we met again, and two years later I married her. Then I learned that she it was, who, knowing nothing about me or even my existence, was responsible for my going to that house where we met.

For fifty-four years she supported my ministry. Not least she rescued me from being too 'booky' a Christian (I was a junior theological tutor at the time) and gently encouraged me to meet people in a parish.

In a way therefore she made me. Are you surprised then if I tell you I believe in the guidance of God: 'My times are in thy hands'?

She died suddenly three weeks ago.

Prayer
*Lord, forgive me if I ever doubt your guidance.*

DCF

153

New Daylight © BRF 1997

**The Bible Reading Fellowship**
Peter's Way, Sandy Lane West, Oxford, OX4 5HG
ISBN 0 7459 3282 7

Distributed in Australia by:
Albatross Books Pty Ltd, PO Box 320, Sutherland,
NSW 2232

Distributed in New Zealand by:
Scripture Union Wholesale, PO Box 760, Wellington

Distributed in South Africa by:
Struik Book Distributors, PO Box 193, Maitland 7405

Distributed in the USA by:
The Bible Reading Fellowship, PO Box M, Winter Park,
Florida 32790

Publications distributed to more than 60 countries

**Acknowledgments**

*Good News Bible* copyright © American Bible Society
1966, 1971 and 1976, published by the Bible Societies
and Collins.

*The Alternative Service Book 1980* copyright © The Central
Board of Finance of the Church of England.

*The Jerusalem Bible* copyright © 1966, 1967 and 1968 by
Darton, Longman & Todd Ltd and Doubleday &
Company, Inc.

*The New Jerusalem Bible* copyright © 1985 by Darton,
Longman & Todd Ltd and Doubleday & Company, Inc.

*The Revised Standard Version of the Bible*, copyright ©
1946, 1952, 1971 by the Division of Christian Education
of the National Council of the Churches of Christ in the
USA.

*The New Revised Standard Version of the Bible*, copyright ©
1989 by the Division of Christian Education of the
National Council of the Churches of Christ in the USA.

*The Holy Bible, New International Version*, copyright ©
1973, 1978, 1984 by International Bible Society. Used
by permission of Hodder & Stoughton Ltd.

*The Holy Bible, New International Reader's Version*,
copyright © 1994 by International Bible Society. Used by
permission of Hodder & Stoughton Ltd, a member of the
Hodder Headline Group. All rights reserved.

*New English Bible* copyright © 1970 by permission of
Oxford and Cambridge University Presses.

*Revised English Bible* copyright © 1989 by permission of
Oxford and Cambridge University Presses.

Cover photograph: Jon Arnold

Printed in Denmark

# SUBSCRIPTION INFORMATION
# & ORDER FORMS

# SUBSCRIPTIONS

## NEW DAYLIGHT—GUIDELINES—LIVEWIRES

Please note our new subscription rates for 1997–1998. From **1 May 1997** the new subscription rates will be:

**Individual Subscriptions** covering 3 issues for under 5 copies, payable in advance (including postage and packing):

|  |  | UK | Surface | Airmail |
|---|---|---|---|---|
| LIVEWIRES (8–10 yr olds) | 3 volumes p.a. | £12.00 | £13.50 | £15.00 |
| GUIDELINES | each set of 3 p.a. | £9.30 | £10.50 | £12.90 |
| NEW DAYLIGHT | each set of 3 p.a. | £9.30 | £10.50 | £12.90 |
| NEW DAYLIGHT LARGE PRINT | each set of 3 p.a. | £15.00 | £18.60 | £21.00 |

**Group Subscriptions** covering 3 issues for 5 copies or more, sent to ONE address (post free):

| | | |
|---|---|---|
| LIVEWIRES | £10.50 | 3 volumes p.a. |
| GUIDELINES | £7.80 | each set of 3 p.a. |
| NEW DAYLIGHT | £7.80 | each set of 3 p.a. |
| NEW DAYLIGHT LARGE PRINT | £13.50 | each set of 3 p.a. |

**Please note that the annual billing period for Group Subscriptions runs from 1 May to 30 April.**

Copies of the notes may also be obtained from Christian bookshops:

| | |
|---|---|
| LIVEWIRES | £3.50 each copy |
| GUIDELINES and NEW DAYLIGHT | £2.60 each copy |
| NEW DAYLIGHT LARGE PRINT | £4.50 each copy |

---

Please note that the Lightning Bolts range also includes volumes of undated daily Bible reading notes for 10–14 year olds. Contact your local bookshop or BRF direct for details.

# SUBSCRIPTIONS

❑ I would like to give a gift subscription (please complete both name and address sections below)
❑ I would like to take out a subscription myself (complete name and address details only once)
❑ Please send me details of Life Membership Subscriptions

This completed coupon should be sent with appropriate payment to BRF. Alternatively, please write to us quoting your name, address, the subscription you would like for either yourself or a friend (with their name and address), the start date and credit card number, expiry date and signature if paying by credit card.

Gift subscription name _____

Gift subscription address _____

_____ Postcode _____

Please send to the above, beginning with the May 1997 issue:

| (please tick box) | UK | SURFACE | AIR MAIL |
|---|---|---|---|
| LIVEWIRES | ❑ £12.00 | ❑ £13.50 | ❑ £15.00 |
| GUIDELINES | ❑ £9.30 | ❑ £10.50 | ❑ £12.90 |
| NEW DAYLIGHT | ❑ £9.30 | ❑ £10.50 | ❑ £12.90 |
| NEW DAYLIGHT LARGE PRINT | ❑ £15.00 | ❑ £18.60 | ❑ £21.00 |

Please complete the payment details below and send your coupon, with appropriate payment to: **The Bible Reading Fellowship, Peter's Way, Sandy Lane West, Oxford OX4 5HG**

Your name _____

Your address _____

_____ Postcode _____

Total enclosed £ _____ (cheques should be made payable to 'BRF')

Payment by cheque ❑ postal order ❑ Visa ❑ Mastercard ❑ Switch ❑

Card number: ☐☐☐☐ ☐☐☐☐ ☐☐☐☐ ☐☐☐☐

Expiry date of card: ☐☐☐☐  Issue number (Switch): ☐☐☐☐

Signature (essential if paying by credit/Switch card) _____

NB: BRF notes are also available from your local Christian bookshop.

ND0197          The Bible Reading Fellowship is a Registered Charity

# BIBLE READING RESOURCES PACK

A pack of resources and ideas to help to promote Bible reading in your church is available from BRF. The pack which will be of use at any time during the year includes sample editions of the notes, magazine articles, leaflets about BRF Bible reading resources and much more. Unless you specify the month in which you would like the pack sent, we will send it immediately on receipt of your order. We greatly appreciate your donations towards the cost of producing the pack (without them we would not be able to make the pack available) and we welcome your comments about the contents of the pack and your ideas for future ones.

This coupon should be sent to:

**The Bible Reading Fellowship**
**Peter's Way**
**Sandy Lane West**
**Oxford OX4 5HG**

Name _____

Address _____

_____

_____ Postcode _____

Please send me _____ Bible Reading Resources Pack(s)

Please send the pack now/ in_____ (month).

I enclose a donation for £_____ towards the cost of the pack.

# BRF PUBLICATIONS ORDER FORM

Please ensure that you complete and send off both sides of this order form.
Please send me the following book(s):

| | | Quantity | Price | Total |
|---|---|---|---|---|
| 2975 | Day by Day with the Psalms (D. Cleverley Ford) | _____ | £5.99 | _____ |
| 3286 | Ultimate Holiday Club Guide (A. Charter/J. Hardwick) | _____ | £9.99 | _____ |
| 2985 | Ultimate Holday Club Cassette (A. Charter/J. Hardwick) (incl VAT) | _____ | £5.99 | _____ |
| 3295 | Livewires: Footsteps and Fingerprints (Sharples) | _____ | £3.50 | _____ |
| 3296 | Livewires: Families and Feelings (Butler) | _____ | £3.50 | _____ |
| 3509 | The Jesus Prayer (S. Barrington-Ward) | _____ | £3.50 | _____ |
| 3298 | Searching for Truth (J. Polkinghorne) | _____ | £6.99 | _____ |
| 3539 | The Apple of His Eye (B. Plass) | _____ | £5.99 | _____ |
| 3253 | The Matthew Passion (J. Fenton) | _____ | £5.99 | _____ |
| 2989 | What's In A Word? (book) (D. Winter) | _____ | £5.99 | _____ |
| 3072 | What's In A Word? (pack) (D. Winter) (incl VAT) | _____ | £9.99 | _____ |
| 2821 | People's Bible Commentary: Genesis (H. Wansbrough) | _____ | £6.99 | _____ |
| 2823 | People's Bible Commentary: Hosea–Micah (J. Tetley) | _____ | £6.99 | _____ |
| 2824 | People's Bible Commentary: Mark (R.T. France) | _____ | £9.99 | _____ |
| 3281 | People's Bible Commentary: Galatians (J. Fenton) | _____ | £6.99 | _____ |
| 3510 | The Unlocking (book) (A. Plass) | _____ | £5.99 | _____ |
| 3512 | The Unlocking (cassette) (A. Plass) (incl VAT) | _____ | £7.99 | _____ |
| 3299 | Forty Days with the Messiah (book) (D. Winter) | _____ | £5.99 | _____ |
| 3542 | Messiah (cassette) (D. Winter/S. Over) (incl VAT) | _____ | £8.99 | _____ |
| 3544 | Forty Days with the Messiah (pack) (D. Winter/S. Over) (incl VAT) | _____ | £13.99 | _____ |
| 2523 | Confirmed for Life (S. Brown/G. Reid) | _____ | £2.99 | _____ |
| 2971 | Feeding on God (S. Brown) | _____ | £2.99 | _____ |
| 2990 | Value Me (book) (S. Brown/P. Lawson Johnson) | _____ | £5.99 | _____ |
| 2991 | Value Me (pack) (S. Brown/P. Lawson Johnson) (incl VAT) | _____ | £13.98 | _____ |
| 2598 | Day by Day Volume 1 (various) | _____ | £10.99 | _____ |
| 2999 | Day by Day Volume 2 (various) | _____ | £9.99 | _____ |
| 3250 | Day by Day Volume 3 (various) | _____ | £10.99 | _____ |

Total cost of books £ _____

Postage and packing (see over) £ _____

TOTAL £ _____

See over for payment details. All prices are correct at time of going to press, are subject to the prevailing rate of VAT and may be subject to change without prior warning.
NB: All BRF titles are also available from your local Christian bookshop.
ND0197          The Bible Reading Fellowship is a Registered Charity

# PAYMENT DETAILS

Please complete the payment details below and send with appropriate payment and completed order form to:

**The Bible Reading Fellowship,**
**Peter's Way,**
**Sandy Lane West,**
**Oxford OX4 5HG**

Name _____

Address _____

_____

_____Postcode _____

Total enclosed £ _____ (cheques should be made payable to 'BRF')

Payment by cheque ❏ postal order ❏ Visa ❏ Mastercard ❏ Switch ❏

Card number: ☐☐☐☐ ☐☐☐☐ ☐☐☐☐ ☐☐☐☐

Expiry date of card: ☐☐☐☐  Issue number (Switch): ☐☐☐☐

Signature (essential if paying by credit/Switch card) _____

| POSTAGE AND PACKING CHARGES | | | |
|---|---|---|---|
| order value | UK | Europe | Surface | Air Mail |
| £6.00 & under | £1.25 | £2.25 | £2.25 | £3.50 |
| £6.01–£14.99 | £3.00 | £3.50 | £4.50 | £6.50 |
| £15.00–£29.99 | £4.00 | £5.50 | £7.50 | £11.00 |
| £30.00 & over | free | prices on request | | |

Alternatively you may wish to order books using the BRF telephone order hotline:
01865 748227

The Bible Reading Fellowship is a Registered Charity